# CLEAN CAKES

# CLEAN CAKES

*Delicious pâtisserie made with whole, natural and nourishing
ingredients and free from gluten, dairy and refined sugar*

**Henrietta Inman**

Photography by Lisa Linder

jacqui
small

First published in 2016 by
Jacqui Small LLP
74–77 White Lion Street
London N1 9PF

Publisher: Jacqui Small
Senior Commissioning Editor: Fritha Saunders
Managing Editor: Emma Heyworth-Dunn
Senior Designer: Rachel Cross
Project Manager and Editor: Claire Wedderburn-Maxwell
Production: Maeve Healy
Photographer: Lisa Linder
Additional photography on pages 70, 73, 95, 120, 146 and 164 by Laura Edwards
Prop Stylists: Cynthia Inions and Henrietta Inman

ISBN: 978 1 910254 38 7

A catalogue record for this book is available
from the British Library.

2018 2017 2016
10 9 8 7 6 5 4 3

Printed in China

# CONTENTS

# INTRODUCTION

*Food is all about pleasure and joy and these are key to* **Clean Cakes**. *Creating nourishing, delicious food to be shared by everyone is one of life's great pleasures. I believe that when we use conscious cooking techniques and unrefined wholefood ingredients, sourced locally, in season and organic when possible, health and happiness is the natural consequence.*

## A NEW PÂTISSERIE

A tea-time loaf brimming with toasted pecans, sticky succulent dates and baked banana; light toffee-flavoured coconut nectar sugar and creamy cashew butter in a soft and mellow butterscotch blondie; honeyed dried fruits, nutty buckwheat and sweet chestnut flours married together in a comforting fruit cake; the distinct crunch of millet flour and freshly dug root vegetables in a divine tart or spiced breakfast muffin … I could quite happily continue lauding the wealth of gloriously delicious and nourishing foods that I use in my pâtisserie today, but my work has not always involved such ingredients.

Fresh from university, I started my apprenticeship as a pastry chef in London. Refined white sugar and flour were at the top of the ingredients list; but I did not question those ingredients then. I wanted to learn the classics, the traditional techniques, the precise and meticulous methods and fine craftsmanship involved in the art of pâtisserie. I wanted to soak up everything there was to know about new flavours, textures and how to present cakes and desserts in the most stunning way possible. Each new kitchen I worked in would bring an abundance of new ideas, exciting flavour combinations and elaborate styles of presentation. I enjoyed every bit of kitchen life, but after years of such an intense work-life, I dreamt of coming home to the Suffolk countryside to start my own business.

Attending local farmers' markets, hosting pop-ups, catering for events and creating bespoke celebration cakes, my work as a self-employed pastry chef proved to be a success. However, after about a year of cooking with the same old white flour and sugar, I thought to myself, why be restricted to these ingredients?

Growing up in the countryside taught me to understand not only the value of local, seasonal and fresh produce but also the importance of eating well and to treasure whole, unrefined and natural ingredients. After all, these are the foods that our bodies thrive on. Now, back in the countryside and cooking in this inspirational environment, these ideas suddenly became more alive to me.

Today, we are conscious of healthy eating more than ever before. We understand the importance of cooking from scratch and that what we put into our bodies has a direct impact on how we feel, look and behave. More and more versatile and varied ingredients are becoming available; and new methods of cooking are being explored involving less meat and, instead, an abundance of vegetables, pulses and wholefoods. We are celebrating a more plant-based approach to cooking, realizing how exciting it can be, with a direct positive influence not only on our health, but animal welfare, sustainability and the environment, too.

This is how I love to eat and I know my friends and family do too. But why does this real food revolution in cooking have to end after the main course? Why, when we've eaten a memorable meal, plentiful in fresh vegetables and other unprocessed ingredients, do we want to follow it up with a pudding packed with refined sugar and flour? Inevitably, after one mouthful, comes the impending guilt that sadly seems to have become synonymous with even the merest thought of having a 'treat' today. I decided to spread this celebration for healthy wholefood eating to the sweeter things in life: to pudding, to tea time, to the cake!

## THE BEGINNING OF *CLEAN CAKES*

One of the things I love about having my own business is meeting my customers and hearing their feedback on my work. When I told them about the new ideas I had for my cakes, I was met with smiles of jubilation, proving what I had hoped – that our new approach to leading healthier lives and mindful eating could be embraced at every meal. A 'clean cake' might sound like a contradiction in terms, but you will see that it's not as impossible as it might seem.

Listening to my customers, I soon realized that most people don't want over-sweet cakes or puddings. I never over-sweetened my bakes anyway, as excessively sweet foods are sickly, unnatural and not at all good for us. Cooking with seasonal and local fruit, I loved to make these natural delights the stars of the show, letting their flavours sing without being masked by too much sugar. This idea would continue into my 'Clean Cakes', but this time using alternative natural sweeteners.

I also became aware of the large number of people with allergies and intolerances or who simply prefer not to eat gluten and dairy. I didn't want to turn customers away, I wanted my cakes to be enjoyed by everyone, so I began to research gluten, dairy and refined sugar and their effects on our wellbeing. At the same time, I started experimenting with gluten-free flours such as brown rice and quinoa; I started tasting unrefined sweeteners like coconut nectar sugar and date syrup, thinking of ingredients they would pair well with. Virgin coconut oil, local extra virgin cold pressed (EVCP) rapeseed oil and nut butters could be used in place of butter and refined vegetable oils. Not only was I learning about the amazing nutritional profiles of these allergy-friendly ingredients, but as I tasted each one, I realized how flavoursome they all were, each with different and distinct nuances. What could be the downside to revolutionizing my pâtisserie with these exceptionally delicious *and* nutritious ingredients, which are also suitable for those suffering from allergies and intolerances?

## A RUDE AWAKENING

Arriving in my kitchen armed with my recipes to develop into my 'Clean Cakes', I couldn't wait to start creating with my newly stocked larder. But adapting my recipes wasn't going to be as straightforward as I had hoped. Gluten is a protein found in certain grains such as wheat. Its 'glue' characteristic is what creates the elasticity in breads and the

structure in cakes, binding ingredients, trapping in air and allowing for that all-important rise. Without gluten, a lot of my first recipe tests were crumbly, dense and a little flat. Butter and sugar also help greatly with structure in baked goods, creating softly textured and moist cakes. It was going to take time to learn how to manipulate my new ingredients to create the best textures possible.

In cooking, texture goes hand in hand with flavour. The main thing about plain (all-purpose) flour, caster (superfine) sugar and butter is that they have very neutral flavours onto which one can quite simply layer fruits, citrus, chocolate and other ingredients. I now needed to consider not only creating a balance between the flavours I was adding to my cakes, but also the varied flavours of my new base ingredients and how they would affect the overall product's taste. Unlike plain (all-purpose) flour, teff flour, for example, is dark in colour and has a slight treacly flavour, which I soon learnt went well with autumn-winter fruits but was also divine with dark (bittersweet) chocolate. EVCP rapeseed oil has a strong flavour compared with butter, but is heavenly in cakes with earthy-tasting root vegetables or in nutritious bars made with grains, seeds and nuts. Different sweeteners would all affect the other flavours in my cakes.

With more and more recipe testing, my confidence in these phenomenal ingredients and my excitement about my new cakes soared. *Clean Cakes* was going to be the

whole package, containing ingredients being used for their flavour, their texture *and* their amazing nutritional profiles, combining them in well thought-out, balanced and memorable cakes and desserts.

Today I have wedded my knowledge as a pastry chef with my passion for alternative, versatile and varied ingredients. I have created over 75 recipes for this book, as well as my foundation recipes, which I hope you will enjoy as much as myself, my family, friends and customers. Knowing I use such powerfully flavoursome and nutritious ingredients makes my job a real joy. Cooking with these ingredients, no thoughts of deprivation, sacrifice or labels should come into play. Instead, my new approach to pâtisserie is about embracing and enjoying wholefood natural ingredients that are delicious *and* good for you, with recipes that will make you smile not just on the outside but the inside, too. After all, the most important part of cooking is to bring happiness to the people who eat your food.

## CLEAN CAKES PHILOSOPHY

*Clean Cakes* is about embracing the skills and techniques I have learnt as a traditional pastry chef and using them to elevate real food ingredients. I want to banish once and for all the misconception that healthy food is bland, colourless or uninspiring. When cooked correctly, it can be exciting,

bright and vibrant, beautiful to look at and eat, and really good for us, too.

Food should never be about deprivation – life is about balance, having your cake and eating it every so often! When food is packed with such nourishing ingredients, we are naturally satisfied much more quickly. Processed cakes and bars are just empty calories that provide us with little sustainable energy. With all my cakes, biscuits (cookies) and bars containing not only low-GI natural sweeteners but also good amounts of fibre, good fats and protein, the sugars they contain are released much more slowly, leaving you feeling sated and full of energy for long periods of time.

*Clean Cakes* also embraces a more alkaline approach to cooking. Acid-forming foods, including all processed foods, cow's dairy, wheat and refined sugar, release acidic residue during digestion, and an excess of acid in our bodies can lead to digestive issues and problems such as lack of energy.

*Clean Cakes* is a cookbook for everyone who enjoys cooking as well as experimenting with new and alternative ingredients. Whether you have cut out gluten, dairy or processed sugar due to allergies, intolerances or a lifestyle choice, *Clean Cakes* is also for you. There are many egg-free recipes suitable for vegans and those with egg allergies, grain-free recipes, and all recipes are soy free, too. For those with nut allergies, recipes can easily be adapted. So let us all get back in the kitchen and eat real food!

# Dairy – the alternatives

*There is a misconception that we need to eat dairy, especially cow's milk, to get sufficient calcium. However, green vegetables, such as broccoli and dark leafy greens, pulses, nuts and seeds are all reliable sources of absorbable calcium.*

## LACTOSE INTOLERANCE AND DAIRY ALLERGIES

Milk allergies or intolerances, also known as dairy intolerance, are especially common among young children but adults suffer from them too. They occur from an allergy to the milk protein, casein, and can cause complaints such as asthma, eczema, sinus issues, acne and constipation. Lactose intolerance, caused by the inability to digest lactose, milk sugar, is widespread and manifests itself in symptoms such as bloating, abdominal pain, wind and diarrhoea.

Dairy is also a source of animal fat, which should be consumed in moderation. If you do consume dairy, choose organic full-fat varieties of milks, yogurts and butters from grass-fed cows, goats or sheep. Raw and unpasteurized varieties can be even better for us, so when possible, choose these over manufactured milk products, which are stripped of a lot of their nutritional value.

## WHAT DOES DAIRY DO IN BAKING?

The majority of baking books use butter, cream and milk as key ingredients. Although convenient and easy, I have realized that there is a baking-life beyond dairy products! Yes, butter, milk or yogurt add a nice softness to baked goods, but there is such a vast number of incredibly delicious, diverse and healthful plant-based dairy-free alternatives we could be using instead.

## DAIRY-FREE ALTERNATIVES TO MILK

### Nut milks and plant-based milks
I use nut milks (see page 28) in my recipes. As well as their reliable calcium content, nuts are rich sources of protein, omega 3 fatty acids, dietary fibre, vitamins and minerals. I mainly use almond and cashew milk as these nuts create softly flavoured products and their relatively neutral creaminess allows for other flavours to be layered easily onto them. I also use specific milks such as hazelnut for a Honey praline ganache (see page 39), or pistachio for a Pistachio crème anglaise (see page 132). In these recipes, I urge you to use the milks suggested, but in the other recipes, where I mainly use almond milk, you can try other similar less strongly flavoured milks. Though I prefer nut

milks, brown rice milk and oat milk would make good alternatives. If you do not make your own plant-based milk, buy varieties that have not been sweetened and do not contain any additives, stabilizers, thickeners and preservatives. See Stockists page 176.

## DAIRY-FREE ALTERNATIVES TO CREAM AND CREAM CHEESE

No more cloying whipped cream and sugary dense icings (frostings) leaving you feeling bloated and tired. Embrace these dreamily light, delicate, flavourful plant-based alternatives.

### Cashew nuts
Their creamy texture and flavour make cashew nuts really useful for dairy-free cooking. After soaking, they can be blended and made into thick cream (see page 27) and milk (see page 28) to be used as ingredients in raw and cooked cakes, icings (frostings), thick sauces or drinks. Cashew nuts help to aid fat metabolism and maintain healthy blood-fat levels and are great for keeping our skin, hair, blood cells and bone marrow in good condition.

### Macadamia nuts
With a milky smooth flavour similar to cashew nuts, they can be soaked and blended to create milks, creams and dairy-free ice cream, like my Bitter chocolate orange ice cream cake (see page 151). They contain healthy fats, antioxidants, iron and zinc.

### Coconut milk
Coconut milk has a relatively light flavour and when well balanced with other ingredients is not at all overpowering, as in my Tiramisù mousse (see page 141). I either use liquid coconut milk, or it can be whipped into a light cream (see page 27) to create delectable mousses, 'cheesecakes' and icings (frostings) for cakes or to serve as an accompaniment. Coconuts are one of the most alkaline-forming foods.

### Avocado
This may seem like an odd dairy alternative, but you can blend its rich and creamy flesh to make a wonderfully light purée, which is easy to add flavours to. As it turns brown with oxidization, you need to add ingredients that deter this and complement its colour, for example lime or mint, or those that conceal oxidization, such as cacao or coffee. Add liquid or whipped coconut cream, blended almonds or cashew nuts and coconut oil to make flavoured creams, icings (frostings), mousses and raw cakes. Avocado is a

good source of healthy-heart fats, protein and almost 20 essential nutrients, such as fibre, B vitamins and vitamin E.

## DAIRY-FREE ALTERNATIVES TO YOGURT AND BUTTERMILK

### My cashew 'yogurt'

Made from blended cashew nuts, this makes an unctuous creamy base onto which numerous flavours can be layered. Like yogurt, it makes an excellent accompaniment to all my bakes, and is great at breakfast too. I call it 'yogurt' due to its yogurt-like consistency, but it does not contain any probiotics (see below). See also cashew nuts (opposite).

### Coconut yogurt

A sublime accompaniment to the recipes in this book, it is so rich that a little goes a very long way so do not be put off by its price. It adds a luxurious creaminess to mousses and icings (frostings) and adds moistness to tea breads and cakes. It is made entirely of freshly squeezed cream from the white flesh of the coconut, rich in minerals and high in fibre.

### Almond milk with apple cider vinegar

This makes a successful substitute for buttermilk. The apple cider vinegar replaces the yogurt-like slightly acidic flavour of buttermilk, as well as reacting with bicarbonate of soda (baking soda) to create a perfect rise, resulting in a light product with a soft milky texture and flavour and a good crust. Apple cider vinegar helps to alkalize the body and aid digestion and metabolism. Opt for unfiltered, unpasteurized varieties 'with the mother' and store in a cool place.

### A note on soya, yogurt and probiotics

I don't use soya for environmental, health and taste reasons. While manufactured yogurts are often seen as a healthy product, there are better sources of calcium and probiotics – for example eating fermented foods and taking a probiotic supplement. (See also Lactose intolerance, opposite.)

## DAIRY-FREE ALTERNATIVES TO BUTTER

### Coconut butter

This is made from the flesh of the coconut meat, while the oil is extracted. Although I prefer to mainly use coconut oil in my cooking, coconut butter, with its buttery consistency as well as no coconut flavour or aroma, is also useful.

### Virgin coconut oil

Antibacterial, antiviral and antifungal, this amazing oil is unrefined and unbleached and can help to control blood sugar levels. It is a stable cooking oil, responding well to heat, and I use it in the majority of my baking and raw desserts and bars. Its subtle coconut flavour is not overpowering, indeed, it has a slight creamy sweetness.

### Extra virgin cold pressed (EVCP) rapeseed oil

With a high smoke point and velvety texture, this is the other oil I use for most of my cooking. It has a distinct, light, nutty flavour, is very versatile, adds depth, and is excellent in cakes, cookies, tea breads and loaves. Avoid cheap rapeseed oils that go through harsh extraction methods. Choose cold pressed oils from non-GM crops, as most are in Britain, as they retain all of their golden yellow colour and great flavour. EVCP rapeseed oil is rich in omega 3 and contains omega 6 and 9, vitamin E and less saturated fat than olive oil. Indeed, more and more chefs are making use of this tasty, heart-healthy oil. If possible, choose local oil.

### Nut butters and seed pastes

These are widely used in *Clean Cakes*, from almond, peanut, hazelnut and cashew butters to pistachio paste and tahini, made from sesame seeds. I use all of these to add their unique flavours to my products. They can also replace butter in biscuits (cookies), either alone or combined with coconut oil, be combined with natural sweeteners to make praline paste for use in cakes and ganaches, and add softness to bakes.

### Cold pressed flax seed oil

With its high omega 3 fatty acid content, cold pressed flax seed oil is one of the best seed oils for cold use only.

### Non-hydrogenated dairy-free butter

Food *must* deliver on flavour, and if I think my cakes taste better with dairy-free butter rather than a plant-based oil, I will use it. Just five times in *Clean Cakes* I use non-hydrogenated dairy-free sunflower butter. It is rich in omega 3 and I always choose brands that are free from artificial colours and preservatives. If you prefer dairy butter, opt for organic from grass-fed cows, goats or sheep.

## DOESN'T CHOCOLATE CONTAIN DAIRY?

*Real* chocolate, not heavily processed milk chocolate and white chocolate (which actually contain hardly any or no cocoa solids at all), should not contain any dairy. All that is necessary is the cocoa butter, cocoa mass and a source of sweetness. I opt for dark (bittersweet) chocolate that is above 75 per cent cocoa solids. See also 'buying chocolate' on page 20, or make your own chocolate (see page 156).

# Sugar – the alternatives

Refined cane sugar is available in many forms. In baking we usually turn to white caster (superfine) and granulated sugar plus icing (confectioner's) sugar. Brown sugars are regularly used too, with a misconception that they are a 'healthier' alternative. All types add sweetness to baked goods, complement and enhance other flavours, as well as helping to create the right texture. But whether white, brown or thick golden syrups, all types of refined sugarcane are stripped of virtually all their vitamins, minerals and fibre. When combined with other highly processed 'empty' ingredients in ready-made manufactured 'food', it causes our blood sugar levels to shoot up and crash down, leaving us feeling cranky, tired and with low energy. When sugars are over-consumed and our bodies cannot use them up, they are converted into fats that get stored around our waists and organs, which can be severely detrimental to our health. A lot of cane sugar production does not support sustainable farming either. So, if it causes us such discomfort, why do we all crave it?

Packaged foods, ready-made sauces, low-fat 'healthy' alternatives and convenient snacks are all packed full of sugar, whether obvious or hidden. People have become so used to tasting sugar that they constantly crave it and want to eat unnaturally over-sweetened foods. If it is processed and not real food, it's probably not good for us, so let's embrace the naturally occurring sugars in seasonal fruits, vegetables and alternative unrefined sweeteners!

## NATURAL SWEETENERS

Let's face it, life would be sad without a birthday cake or a pudding after Sunday lunch, but you *can* have your cake and eat it! I take advantage of natural sweeteners for their extraordinary and unique flavours and nutrient-richness. Combined with other wholefood ingredients, abundant in protein, good fats and fibre, they provide sustained energy and a proper satisfaction that comes with eating real food.

I do take into account that although the natural sweeteners are unprocessed, they are still forms of sugar, which can disrupt the body's balance, so should be used and eaten in moderation. I add sweetness when necessary, I add less when I think I can. If you make anything in *Clean Cakes* and it doesn't satisfy your sweet preference, add more or less sugar when you next make it, or add a drizzle of honey, coconut nectar or maple syrup after baking. After all, sweetness is a matter of personal taste.

All these sugars have very different flavours and consistencies so I would recommend sticking to the recipes for the best results. If you want to try another sweetener, note that it may affect the overall flavour and texture.

### Honey substitute for vegans

Apart from honey, all of the natural sweeteners I have listed are suitable for vegans. If you are a vegan, try replacing the honey with your preferred plant-based liquid sweetener. In my opinion, coconut nectar is the best replacement, but use what suits your tastes best.

## CRYSTALLIZED NATURAL SWEETENERS

### Coconut sugar/Coconut nectar sugar

Probably the natural sweetener I use the most as it creates the lightest baked goods. Also known as coconut nectar, palm or blossom sugar, and with no actual coconut flavour, it has a mellow caramel-toffee flavour and colour that is well suited to most ingredients. It can be used instead of caster (superfine) sugar, substituting equal amounts of coconut sugar or reducing it and combining it with other natural sweeteners like apple purée. It has a low GI rating of 35 and is a natural source of trace nutrients like iron, magnesium, potassium, zinc and amino acids. It is made from 100 per cent coconut blossom sap from the coconut palm tree, extracted and sustainably produced using a time-honoured traditional practice. Buy organic, unrefined, unfiltered, unbleached varieties containing no additives or preservatives.

### Palmyra nectar powder (SugaVida)

This is the most phenomenal superfood sweetener! Harvested from the blossom of the Palmyra tree, it is grown sustainably in south-east India. A unique alkaline sweetener that has a 5000-year heritage in Ayurvedic medicine, Palmyra nectar powder has a low GI of 40 and contains over 15 essential vitamins and minerals including bioavailable B12, iron, potassium and magnesium. Dark in colour, with a slightly rich caramel taste, it works best in recipes that call for brown sugar. I like to use it with autumn fruits, spices and dark (bittersweet) chocolate. With its rich sweetness, you can use 30–50 per cent less than if using processed sugar. Buy organic and avoid blocks of 'jaggery' sold in Indian food markets.

## LIQUID NATURAL SWEETENERS

### Raw honey

Choose local, unpasteurized honey that has not been heated over 45°C (113°F) (unlike most honeys on sale in supermarkets which have been heat-treated and contain additives). Raw honey is antibacterial, antifungal and a powerful antioxidant, retaining most of its nutrients, such as vitamins B6 and C, and can help to reduce inflammation. It has incredible depth of flavour, changing from hive to hive. As with many of my natural sweeteners, a little goes a long way and honey is very sweet (it has a GI of 50). Thanks to its relatively delicate flavour, it generally goes well with most ingredients. I use it in some baked products, but to get the most out of its rich nutrient content, I mainly use it raw, in creams and desserts, or add a drizzle as a finishing touch.

### Coconut nectar/Coconut nectar syrup

Like coconut sugar (see opposite), this is made from coconut blossom sap, which has not been pollinated so is suitable for vegans. The sap is evaporated over an open fire to concentrate its natural sweetness and form a runny syrup, which is then cooled and bottled. There are no other added ingredients in 100 per cent pure coconut nectar. It has a more delicate and slightly fragrant flavour than coconut sugar. It is slightly less sweet than honey so I use it to add subtle sweetness to creams, baked goods and raw desserts. Colours vary from blonde to dark, as with the sugar, so when using with lighter ingredients, like coconut cream, opt for light (blonde) nectar if possible.

### Maple syrup

Made from the concentrated sap of the Canadian maple tree, it contains minerals such as iron, zinc, manganese and potassium and has a GI rating of 54. Its deep burnt toffee-caramel flavour makes it good for topping pancakes and porridge, but it is also great in baked goods. It goes well with nuttier tasting flours like buckwheat, brown rice and teff, root vegetables and spices. Avoid 'maple flavoured syrup'. I prefer to use the darker Grade B maple syrup as it has a stronger flavour than Grade A, so you can use less.

### Date syrup

Opt for organic and unsweetened varieties. See dates and date syrup (below).

## CLEVER SWEETENERS

### Dates and date syrup

Sticky dates are great added to raw desserts or cereal bars, adding sweetness and helping ingredients stick together. Whole dates and date syrup have a strong treacly sweet flavour, which marries well with dark (bittersweet) chocolate, nuts, bananas and most gluten-free flours.

Dates vary hugely in sweetness and texture so try to buy the best-quality, really sweet and plump dates. If they are a little dry, soak them in warm water for 30 minutes to 1 hour until soft. Medjool dates are the sweetest, softest and most plump dates you can buy, which means they blend, process and bind well and create the tastiest results.

### Dried fruits

A great source of dietary fibre, dried fruits contain many nutrients, vitamins and minerals. As well as dates, I use dried figs, apricots, sour cherries, currants, raisins, blueberries, goji berries, white mulberries and cranberries in *Clean Cakes*. When using them I take into account their high sweetness levels, reducing the other sweeteners I add. If the fruit is dry, soak in warm water or tea for about 10 minutes. Buy unwaxed, unsweetened and unsulphured varieties.

### Fresh fruits

Fruits add a lot of their natural sweetness to cakes. Mashed bananas are great added to muffins, and apple purée (see page 32) is especially useful in my *Clean Cakes*. I often use it with another sweetener, such as Palmyra nectar powder or maple syrup, and it creates the perfect balance of sweetness. See also Veganism and egg replacements on page 18.

### Vegetables

Do not underestimate the power of sweet vegetables! Squash, especially sweeter varieties, can be cooked and puréed and added to bakes, with very little other sweetness needed, as in my Baked kabocha squash pie (see page 135). Similarly, pumpkin purée, carrots and parsnips add sweetness to cakes and muffins.

## SWEET FLAVOUR BOOSTERS

### Spices

The flavour and nutritional potency of spices can sometimes be overlooked but they can really make dishes come alive. Many have intoxicatingly sweet aromas as well as being health-promoting, like cinnamon and cardamom, ginger and nutmeg. Instead of using sugar on porridge, try a blend of spices like fennel seed, cinnamon, cardamom and cloves.

### Vanilla

I use pure unsweetened vanilla extract and vanilla seeds, scraped out of the vanilla pod (bean). Vanilla is a very versatile flavouring, adding depth to other flavours or acting as a flavour on its own. Its mellow richness enhances recipes that need a little extra sweetness. Pair it with almost everything from chocolate or rhubarb to lemon or coconut. Don't throw away empty vanilla pods (beans). Store them in a jar then use to flavour baked fruits, smoothies or granola.

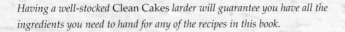

Having a well-stocked **Clean Cakes** larder will guarantee you have all the ingredients you need to hand for any of the recipes in this book.

1. Date syrup
2. Coconut flour
3. Macadamia nuts
4. Almond butter
5. Cashew butter
6. Whipped coconut cream
7. Millet
8. Quinoa
9. Short-grain brown rice

10. Palmyra nectar powder
11. Cashew nuts
12. Teff flour
13. Coconut sugar
14. Virgin coconut oil
15. EVCP rapeseed oil
16. Raw honey
17. Cinnamon stick
18. Vanilla pods (beans)

# Gluten – the alternatives

*Gluten is a protein found in many grains, the most common known being wheat, but it is also in spelt, kamut, durum, rye and barley.*

## GLUTEN SENSITIVITY AND COELIAC DISEASE

We cannot ignore the number of people suffering from gluten sensitivity nowadays. Indeed, possibly as many as one in ten are sensitive to gluten. Gluten sensitivity or intolerance, where gluten acts as an irritant to the digestive tract, can manifest itself in digestive problems causing flatulence and bloating, but also symptoms like acne, fatigue and depression. In the most extreme cases, people suffer from a permanent intolerance to gluten, known as coeliac disease, an autoimmune disease that causes inflammatory damage to the small intestine, leading to vitamin and mineral deficiencies and bowel problems.

It seems to me to be no coincidence that this prevalence in gluten sensitivity and coeliac disease goes hand in hand with the hybridization of wheat and many other gluten-containing cereal crops today. No longer like the grains that our ancestors once ate, many crops are being genetically modified, sprayed with large amounts of chemicals to produce higher yields and becoming stripped of nearly all of their nutritional content. With the huge increase in gluten levels in modern wheat and the fact that we are consuming more grains than ever, scientists are now linking today's intensive farming methods and our current eating habits with the surge in gluten sensitivities and coeliac disease.

So, why do we rely on wheat, found in white bread, cereals and shop-bought pastries and cookies, when there are numerous other gloriously delicious nutrient-dense grains available today? It might seem hard to approach baking with another ingredient when refined white wheat flour is what we are used to, but I will show you that it is not only easy, but also incredibly delicious *and* good for you to cook with alternative and exciting gluten-free grains.

## WHAT DOES GLUTEN DO?

Gluten comes from the Latin word meaning 'glue', and in bread, cakes and pastry, that is exactly what it does. It binds ingredients together, trapping in air to create elasticity in dough, helping breads and cakes to keep their shape, light texture and structure. The sheer strength of gluten is best illustrated when it has been overworked or has not had time to rest, resulting in tough unappealing bread, a heavy cake or chewy pastry.

## COMBINING GLUTEN-FREE FLOURS AND STARCHES

If you don't use gluten you might worry about your crumb being too short, your tart case collapsing or your cake not being tender, but don't! The most important thing to remember in gluten-free baking is that combining flours, often with starches, as opposed to using just one gluten-free flour, is the key to creating the best possible textures. Replacing wheat flour with exactly the same amount of brown rice flour, for example, will give a heavy unappealing result. But, combining brown rice flour with buckwheat flour and a little arrowroot starch will allow for a better product. Combining flours also adds variety and improved nutrient profiles, not to mention great depth of flavour. I create different blends for all my products, so use the combination of flours and starches in this book as a guide to creating your own gluten-free flour blends.

## GLUTEN-FREE STARCHES AND BAKING AIDS

We need to replace the ingredient-binding properties of gluten with gluten-free starches such as arrowroot, cornflour (cornstarch) and gram flour. These natural starches are used only in small amounts, when necessary, to help ingredients bind, to lighten products and to enhance their overall texture. You can leave them out if you prefer, replacing them with the same quantities of the other flours in the recipe, just be aware that the texture of your end product might be altered.

### Arrowroot, cornflour (cornstarch) and gram flour
I use arrowroot as the main binding starch in the vast majority of my cakes as it is the most easily digestible starch. For some recipes, a combination of flours (seen in almost all of my cakes) as well as a combination of starches is necessary. In such cases, I combine arrowroot with either cornflour (cornstarch), the white starch isolated from the whole corn kernel, or gram flour, a rich yellow flour made from skinned and finely milled chickpeas, which is a staple in Indian cuisine. Gram flour is high in protein, which helps ingredients to bind and rise, and is a useful egg substitute.

### Baking powder and bicarbonate of soda (baking soda)
Both create a good rise and add lightness, while bicarbonate of soda (baking soda) also helps to add a slight crisp crust in some bakes. Use gluten-free varieties.

### Xanthan gum and guar gum
I try to avoid using gums, but sometimes (in four recipes) a little extra help with binding is necessary. Only small

amounts are needed as they are very effective. They create a good rise in baked goods and are therefore useful in vegan/egg-free baking. Use gluten-free varieties.

## WHOLEGRAIN GLUTEN-FREE FLOURS AND GRAIN-FREE FLOURS

Flour plays many roles in baking, providing structure, texture and flavour, as well as adding nutritional value. A huge variety of gluten-free flours and grains are used in *Clean Cakes*, with each flour providing its own characteristics. Please note that all the flours used in the recipes are wholegrain gluten-free flours, containing all of their goodness. All these flours contain high proportions of important vitamins and minerals, fibre, protein, iron and complex carbohydrates, which provide sustained energy.

Whether as flours, flakes or whole grains, they are all great additions to any diet. I prefer not to use bought gluten-free flour blends as they tend to be stripped of most of their nutritional substance, and can contain additives and stabilizers. People who prefer to avoid grains should opt for ground nuts, nut flours and coconut flour. Also see pseudocereals (overleaf).

### Brown rice flour
This has a richer flavour than refined wheat flour thanks to the healthy bran it contains, but it is still a relatively neutral-flavoured flour, and is a good flour to experiment with when gluten-free baking. It aids calcium absorption, is high in vitamin B and rich in manganese. It combines well with buckwheat and teff flours and a little arrowroot. I also use brown rice flakes and wholegrain brown rice.

### Chestnut flour (grain free)
Milled from dried chestnuts, this has a rich, sweet and nutty flavour. It has a fine texture so it needs less coarse flours, like rice, buckwheat or sorghum, to lighten it. Chestnuts are chiefly made of starch, but they are still good sources of minerals, vitamins, protein and fibre.

### Coconut flour (grain free)
With the growing interest in grain-free diets, many people are starting to bake with coconut flour. High in fibre (it contains more than wheat bran), it is lower in carbohydrates than soya and nut flours. Though expensive, a little goes a long way as the flour expands enormously when baked, increasing the yield of baked goods by up to 50 per cent. It has a naturally creamy colour and sweet flavour, with a very slight coconut taste, which goes well with chocolate and vanilla.

### Ground nuts (grain free)
Nuts are alkaline, high in beneficial monounsaturated fats and contain vitamin E, magnesium and potassium. A good source of plant-based protein, you will find whole and ground nuts in a lot of my *Clean Cakes* as they add flavour, great texture and their slight oiliness adds moisture and softness. To grind your own nuts, simply process them in a blender until fine crumbs form, taking care not to over blend and create too much of an oily flour.

### Millet flour
A very soft flour, which imparts a slight sandy crunch and sweet nutty flavour to baked goods. It is best combined with lighter flours like brown rice and buckwheat. Ground from the small round yellow seeds of a cereal grass, it is filling and easy to digest. I use millet flakes in my cereal bars.

### Oat flour
This wholesome flour is beautiful to bake with, imparting a soft light texture to cakes and a crumbliness to biscuits (cookies). As well as helping to lower levels of cholesterol and being beneficial for people with diabetes, oats contain calcium, potassium and fatty acids. I also use rolled oats and sprouted oats in *Clean Cakes*. Buy gluten-free varieties.

### Polenta (cornmeal)
Milled from dried corn kernels, polenta (cornmeal) has a rich yellow colour and its characteristic coarse 'nibbly' texture combines well with brown rice flour to add new dimensions to cakes and muffins. It is a carbohydrate rich in vitamins A, B and E, polyunsaturated fat and other fatty acids, and many minerals such as magnesium and phosphorous. For best results in baking, choose fine 'quick-cook' polenta (cornmeal).

### Sorghum flour
Also known as 'sweet' white sorghum flour, this is a staple food in India and Africa. High in antioxidants, the starch and protein in sorghum take longer than other similar products to digest, so it is particularly helpful for those with diabetes. Sorghum is very different to other wholegrain gluten-free flours, with a soft smooth texture and mild taste, and works well in light sponge cakes.

### Teff flour
Teff is a tiny grain from a type of grass, which we should use more as it provides nine times more iron than wheat does and five times more potassium and calcium than other cereal grains. It is a real flavour and texture enhancer, with its mild sweet-molasses taste and slightly coarse feel.

## PSEUDOCEREALS: *AMARANTH, BUCKWHEAT AND QUINOA*

Rather than being grains, these cereals are more like seeds, and many people who find more commonly consumed grains like oats hard to digest, can find that these seeds suit them better. In their wholegrain form, all can be enjoyed in savoury and sweet dishes such as salads and porridge.

### Amaranth

Amaranth was a staple in the Aztec, Mayan and Incan diets. High in fibre, iron, protein and lysine with a great nutty and earthy flavour, I use amaranth in its wholegrain form, rather than as a flour, because I love the texture of the small pale seeds.

When heated with moisture, the starch in the grain is activated, creating a gelatinous and viscous porridge-like mix, which is delicious as it is, but also helps to bind ingredients in cakes, muffins and breads, which is especially helpful in gluten-free baking.

### Buckwheat

With its wholesome nutty flavour and distinct slightly grainy texture, buckwheat flour is one of my favourite flours to bake with. It comes from a seed related to the rhubarb, sorrel and knotweed plants and combines well with brown rice flour and chestnut flour to achieve the right crumb and flavour.

A complex carbohydrate containing protein, vitamin A, selenium and rutin, a substance that protects the heart, buckwheat is incredibly versatile. I also use buckwheat in its wholegrain form, buckwheat groats, which add crunch to breads, muffins and raw tart bases, and as buckwheat flakes, a bit like oats, in energy bars and porridge.

### Quinoa

Though I generally cook a lot with wholegrain quinoa, another ancient staple of the Incas, I only use quinoa flour and quinoa flakes in my *Clean Cakes*. The flour has a slightly grassy flavour which I find works best in savoury bakes like bread. Arguably the most nutritious grain, it has 60 per cent more protein than wheat and barley, and is rich in minerals such as copper, iron and zinc.

Wholegrain quinoa is a great alternative to couscous and bulgar wheat in everyday cooking served alongside dishes or added into salads. It makes delicious porridge too.

## VEGANISM AND EGG REPLACEMENTS

In *Clean Cakes* you will find many vegan recipes. As my recipes are dairy-free, vegan just means that they are egg-free too and therefore completely free from animal products. These recipes are also suitable for those suffering from egg allergies.

Though eggs are very important in baking, adding rise, lightness, moisture and binding ingredients, effective plant-based alternatives do exist. Look out for recipes using chia seeds, milled flax seeds and psyllium husk powder as the main binding agents instead of eggs.

### Chia seeds and milled flax seeds

Both milled flax seeds and chia seeds have mucilaginous qualities, meaning that they swell up in liquids, creating thick gelatinous binding gels. This is particularly useful in vegan baking where egg would normally help to stick ingredients together.

As a rough guide, 1 egg is the equivalent of 3 tbsp water or plant-based milk mixed with 1 tbsp whole chia seeds or milled flax seeds. Both seeds are extremely nutritious, high in essential fats, fibre and protein. In my baking, I use milled flax seeds more than chia seeds as I have found that they create the best texture and results.

### Psyllium husk powder

This is made from the seeds of a native plant from India and Pakistan. The seeds are hygroscopic, which allows them to expand and become mucilaginous like chia seeds and milled flax seeds.

I use the powder in savoury vegan baking as it has quite a strong flavour and dark colour. Its binding power not only helps to replace the egg, but also the gluten, as the husk binds moisture and helps to make products less crumbly. As a source of soluble dietary fibre, it can be used to relieve constipation.

### Apple purée

Adds sweetness and can help compensate for the moisture lost when baking without eggs. See easy apple purée on page 32.

### Apple cider vinegar and bicarbonate of soda (baking soda)

An effective combination in egg-free baking. See also page 11.

### Gram flour, xanthan gum and guar gum

See pages 16–17.

# Flavour enhancers and superfoods

*To our wonderful base ingredients, seasonal fruits and vegetables are added to create the final products. The following ingredients then take things up a notch, adding fabulous bursts of flavour and nutrients in bucketloads!*

### Cacao butter (theobroma oil)
Cacao butter is the creamy fat part that is separated from the cacao solids of the cacao bean and contains a variety of essential fatty acids. Cocoa butter used in commercial dark (bittersweet) chocolate is slightly processed cacao butter.

### Cacao
Cacao was not named the 'Food of the Gods' by the Mayans and Aztecs for nothing! Cacao is packed full of health-promoting compounds, is a rich source of antioxidants, and helps to eliminate toxins from the body. It also contains iron, magnesium, vitamin C, manganese, copper, fibre, omega 6 fatty acids and theobromine. I use raw cacao in two forms in *Clean Cakes*.

Cacao nibs are the unprocessed, raw, crunchy pieces of the dried raw cacao bean before it is ground. Cacao nibs are great ingredients, or sprinkled on desserts for a final touch.

Cacao powder is made from dried ground cacao beans. It is a pure product unlike cocoa powder, which is heat-refined and can contain sweeteners, milk powders and other artificial additives.

### Carob powder
Carob is higher in natural sugar and lower in fat than cacao. It has a similar taste to chocolate, though it is sweeter with a malty flavour. It is made from the dried pulp of the carob or locust bean. Rich in phosphorous, calcium and vitamin E, carob also acts as an antioxidant and can improve digestion.

### Citrus fruits
Citrus fruits, especially the zest, are very useful additions to baking, balancing out sweetness, adding freshness and complementing flavours.

### Eggs
Always buy free-range eggs, local and organic if possible. Key baking ingredients, they are also incredibly nutritious wholefoods, packed with protein, vitamins and omega 3 fats, as well as dietary cholesterol, calcium and zinc.

### Flowers and flower waters
I use these in a number of ways to add delicately sweet notes to many of my cakes. Fresh petals and flowers add beautiful final touches to cakes, as well as exciting flavours. When dried, they can be ground and added to chocolate truffles or biscuit (cookie) dough. For stronger concentrated floral flavours, I use rosewater and orange blossom water, which add Middle Eastern scents to my cakes and are lovely added to lightly cooked fruits in compotes.

### Herbs
Herbs are full of vitamins and goodness and can really lift up and complement the flavours in a cake or a biscuit (cookie), like in my Courgette (zucchini), basil, lime and pistachio cake (see page 36).

### Himalayan pink salt and coarse sea salt
Salt is so important as it makes flavours come alive. I use Himalayan pink salt for its milder flavour and coarse sea salt when I feel my recipes need that extra edge. Himalayan pink salt is one of the purest forms of salt on earth, free from toxins and rich in vitamins and minerals, as is sea salt.

### Lucuma powder
Lucuma is a Peruvian fruit prized for both its flavour and nutritional profile. It contains a range of vitamins and nutrients, especially beta carotene, and is rich in dietary fibre. A great natural sweetener with a delicate sweet, malty and slightly carrot-orange flavour, it perfectly complements the flavours in cacao, maca and carob so I love adding it to raw chocolate and hot cacao as well as cashew 'yogurt'.

### Maca powder
Maca powder is nutrient-dense and has a slightly stronger flavour than lucuma, so don't add too much! It is similarly malty and caramel-sweet, but can become slightly bitter if over-used. Its light toffee notes are great with cacao.

### Nuts and seeds
Whether used whole, blended into milk, processed into butter, ground into flour or toasted and chopped, nuts and seeds are some of the most flavoursome and nourishing ingredients in my *Clean Cakes*. I recommend activating them, see page 25, to get maximum nutritional benefits.

### Teas
Containing powerful antioxidants and helping to protect against heart disease, both black and green teas are used in *Clean Cakes*. A simple blend of black tea is great for plumping up dried fruits, adding a little flavour too. I also like to pick specific teas for their rich distinctive flavours like chai tea in my Extra fruity fruit loaf (see page 77).

# Stocking your Clean Cakes larder

*If your cupboards and freezer are properly stocked and organized, you will be equipped to embrace wholefood natural cooking and you and your family will reap the benefits.*

### Know your raw materials

There is no question that the better the raw materials, the more stunning the outcome. Quality goes hand in hand with knowing where your food comes from and how it has been grown. Aim for home-grown naturally farmed food whenever possible. When it comes to fresh ingredients, always try to buy local and seasonal or grow your own. If your fruits, vegetables and herbs have travelled less, they are going to taste better, contain their maximum amount of nutrients and look more appealing, vibrant, plump and fresh.

Choose organic when possible. Organic farming is sustainable and therefore better for the environment as well as your body. Whenever possible I opt for fair trade products. Please do not see local, natural and organic produce as 'superior', strange or exclusive when it is better for the earth, better for you and, above all, it is natural!

In particular, buy organic varieties of thin-skinned produce, like apples and berries, where you will be eating the skin. Organic or not, always wash fresh fruit and vegetables before use.

With flours, sweeteners, fats and oils, I buy local or organic so I know they are free from chemical residues and genetic modification.

In my recipes I use my homemade chocolate (see page 156), which is 80% cacao solids. If short on time or ingredients, you can use bought dark (bittersweet) chocolate. The ideal replacement for my homemade chocolate is 85% dark (bittersweet) chocolate as it is the most widely available and has the best results in my recipes. When you buy chocolate, check the ingredients: only cocoa beans or mass, cocoa butter and a little cane sugar should be listed. Opt for organic and fair trade bars when possible.

Practice mindfulness. Local, seasonal and unrefined foods are more densely packed with flavour *and* goodness than mass-produced foods and you will be sated more quickly. Mindful eating encapsulates the whole process, not just the eating, but your awareness of the raw ingredients, their careful preparation and the final dish, which should be truly appreciated and, most importantly, enjoyed!

### Stocking up

Nuts, seeds, dried fruits, flours, grains and sweeteners are all much cheaper if bought in bulk. With some research, shopping wisely and my Stockists list on page 176, you can buy the best-quality produce without spending a fortune. Having a well-stocked larder is a great investment, saving time and money, wasting less and improving your health.

Make the most of the abundance of fruits and vegetables each season and stock up your freezer. Make apple and other fruit purées in the colder months, wash and prepare berries and other fruits during the rest of the year and then freeze everything. With a stocked freezer, you'll be well equipped with ingredients for all the recipes in this book. This will also save you money as buying fresh produce out of season is expensive, not to mention flavourless!

### Storage

When storing ingredients, I prefer to use glass rather than plastic containers, as plastic contains harmful chemicals such as BPA. Empty jam (jelly) jars, bottles and clear glass containers in all shapes and sizes are very useful for storage.

*Flours and sweeteners* Store flours in airtight glass jars in dry cupboards or larders at room temperature. Store liquid sweeteners in the bottles or containers that they are bought in. Always be aware of use-by dates.

*Nuts and seeds* Stored as they are bought, or activated and dried and stored in glass jars (see page 25), nuts and seeds should be kept in the fridge.

*Oils, fats and chocolate* Store in cool places, away from heat and sun. Chocolate, coconut oil and coconut butter can be stored in the fridge in hotter months. Nut and seed butters are best kept in the fridge.

*Spices, extracts and flower waters* Store in airtight jars, in a cool dry cupboard and be aware of use-by dates.

*Vanilla pods (beans)* Keep in an airtight container in a cool, dry place away from heat or light, but do not refrigerate. Well-stored vanilla will keep indefinitely, but still be aware of the use-by date. Do not refrigerate.

# Cook's notes

*Here are my most important points for approaching the recipes in this book. Above all, please read each recipe through carefully before starting. When it comes to baking, precision is key.*

### Oven

All recipes were tested in a convection fan-assisted oven. In general, conventional ovens may need to be set at 10–20°C (25–50°F) hotter (no more) than a convection oven, and the bake time could be slightly longer. Cooking times and temperatures are a guide and should be altered according to the manufacturer's instructions.

Always preheat the oven so it reaches the required temperature before baking. Bake in the centre of the oven for evenness. Halfway through baking, turn the product.

### Measuring

Follow all measurements with maximum accuracy. Use scales, preferably electronic, and proper measuring spoons. Unless specified, all spoon measurements are level.

### Citrus fruits

Always buy unwaxed varieties, preferably organic.

### Dates/Medjool dates

All weights given are for pitted dates (without the stones).

### Eggs

All recipes use large eggs. Use eggs at room temperature.

### Filtered water

When activating nuts, seeds, grains and pseudocereals or soaking dried fruit, milled flax seeds or chia seeds, use filtered water if possible.

### Flours

All flours used are wholegrain.

### Toasting nuts

Most of my recipes call for toasted nuts as toasting 'tickles' out the flavour, making a real difference to the final product. If you prefer your nuts raw, just skip this step. Different nuts vary in toasting time, but I toast most for about 7 minutes.

Toast until the nuts are fragrant, warm to the touch and if you like a toasted flavour, slightly goldening. Harder nuts like almonds and hazelnuts particularly benefit from colour.

## *Equipment*

**Baking parchment** – preferably unbleached.

**Blender** – as powerful as possible. Indispensable for making ground nut flours, nut milks, sauces and raw cake fillings.

**Chopping/cutting boards** – choose wooden rather than plastic.

**Dehydrator** – for drying activated nuts, seeds and buckwheat groats, and for use in raw food 'cooking', such as making raw crackers.

**Food processor** – invest in a good hard-wearing one. Perfect for fine and coarse chopping, emulsions and grinding and binding ingredients for raw tart bases and bars.

**Freestanding or hand-held mixer** – great for easy whisking and mixing with whisk and paddle attachments.

**Graters** – microplane for finely grating citrus zests; box grater for grating vegetables.

**Hand-held/stick blender** – useful for making smooth sauces, creams and ganaches.

**Kitchen scales** – use digital/electric scales for accuracy.

**Knives** – have a set of sharp knives for chopping and a small step-palette knife (frosting spatula) for spreading out cake mix, icings (frostings) and jams (jellies).

**Nut milk bag** – to filter the smooth nut milks used in *Clean Cakes* recipes. Wash and dry after each use.

**Pyrex, glass, ceramic or metal bowls and measuring jugs** – use these rather than plastic.

**Saucepans** – choose cast-iron or stainless steel saucepans (I like heavy-bottomed ones), rather than synthetically coated non-stick saucepans.

**Selection of baking tins** – see recipes for size details.

**Spatulas** – silicone spatulas for folding and scraping.

**Teaspoon and tablespoon set (metric)** – use for maximum accuracy and consistency.

*Some ingredients in my larder. Top shelf left to right: amaranth, dried camomile flowers, Medjool dates, cacao nibs (top), popcorn kernels (bottom), bee pollen, goji berries, Himalayan pink salt, gluten-free oats, buckwheat flakes. Bottom shelf left to right: cinnamon sticks (top), white mulberries (bottom), Incan berries (top), whole star anise (bottom), coconut flakes, hulled hemp seeds, dried chickpeas, millet flakes.*

# FOUNDATION RECIPES

*From preparing your nuts, seeds, grains and pseudocereals to make the most of their nutritive values, to making unctuous creams to accompany your cakes; from homemade nut milks and butters to raw and cooked jams (jellies), these recipes will prove to be invaluable.*

## Soaking and dehydrating

Soaking nuts, seeds, grains and pulses has many benefits for both health and taste. Soaking (or activating) maximizes their flavour, making them sweeter and less bitter, as well as unlocking nutrients for easier absorption.

Anti-nutrients, found in the hulls and outer skins of nuts, seeds, grains and pulses in the form of phytates, or phytic acid, deplete our body of nutrients as they bind with vital nutrients like calcium, iron and zinc and lower their absorption. Soaking reduces the phytic acid, unlocking these nutrients and increasing their availability to the body, as well as neutralizing enzyme inhibitors, which interfere with effective digestion and also deplete our body of nutrients. Soaking therefore makes food much easier to digest and reduces the chance of bloating. Adding a small amount of salt or acidic liquid helps to further neutralize enzyme inhibitors and reduce phytic acid.

In raw recipes, for creams in cakes and 'yogurts', it is of utmost importance to soak the nuts in the recipe to achieve the correct smooth consistency. Once you're in the swing of things, soaking will become an easy habit.

A small amount of phytic acid is okay, so do not worry if you do not have 'activated dried' nuts and seeds as regular nuts and seeds will still work in cooked recipes and recipes for raw cake bases and bars.

### SOAKING

As a general guide, soak nuts, seeds, pseudocereals, grains or pulses in about double the volume of water. For nuts and seeds, add about 1 tsp of salt per 500 ml (17 fl oz / 2⅛ cup). For pseudocereals and grains, add about 1 tsp of lemon juice or apple cider vinegar per 500 ml (17 fl oz / 2⅛ cup).

Timings are a guide, but try not to exceed 12 hours' soaking time as you will wash away oils and nutrients.

250 g (8¾ oz) nuts, seeds, pseudocereals, grains or pulses
500 ml (17 fl oz / 2⅛ cup) filtered water or extra to cover
1 tsp Himalayan pink salt or 1 tsp acidic liquid (see above)

In a glass or ceramic bowl, soak any of the above in the measured water, salt or acidic liquid for the required time (see below). Drain and rinse thoroughly in fresh filtered water, then follow the recipe instructions. It is best to use soaked nuts and seeds immediately but they can be stored in the fridge for a few days, dehydrated or frozen.

### Soaking nuts and seeds

Almonds and hazelnuts are hard nuts and should be soaked for 8–12 hours or overnight. Walnuts, pistachio nuts and pecans are slightly softer, so should be soaked for 6–8 hours. Cashew nuts are even softer and should be soaked for 3–4 hours. Most agree that Brazil nuts, macadamia nuts and pine nuts do not need soaking.

Pumpkin and sunflower seeds should be soaked for 8 hours. Flax, sesame and poppy seeds should be soaked for 8 hours, but you will need a very fine sieve for rinsing them. If you don't have one, then use them raw. I soak chia seeds and milled flax seeds (linseeds) but do not drain them, using the gel formed to bind ingredients. Hulled hemp seeds do not require soaking.

### Soaking pseudocereals, grains and pulses

Amaranth, buckwheat and quinoa and grains such as millet and rice are best soaked for 8–12 hours or overnight.

Pulses such as lentils, chickpeas and dried beans are best soaked for 12 hours or overnight.

### 'ACTIVATED DRIED' NUTS, SEEDS AND GROATS

Some recipes call for 'activated dried' nuts, seeds or buckwheat groats. This is for a crunchy texture and for shelf life. They will taste less bitter and be easier to digest, too.

To dehydrate activated nuts, seeds and buckwheat groats, use a dehydrator set at 45°C / 113°F and dry for 12–48 hours, depending on their size and the quantity. If you do not have a dehydrator, set your oven to the lowest temperature and check the nuts or seeds every few hours.

I dry harder and larger nuts like almonds and walnuts for up to 48 hours and smaller seeds and buckwheat groats for about 24 hours. I recommend tasting them to test if they are ready. If they are crunchy and dry, they are ready to be stored in the fridge in sealed glass jars. Activated dried buckwheat groats can be stored in a sealed jar in a larder or cupboard.

# Basic Nut Butters

A lot of recipes for nut butters add extra oils, but I like my nut butter to be 100 per cent nuts! To achieve the right consistency without using extra liquid, all you need is nuts, a food processor and, most importantly, time. The small amount of heat from the motor of the food processor helps the nuts to release their oils, grinding them down into a thick nutty paste. It's so satisfying to make and tastes so delicious that you'll never use a shop-bought version again.

In my cakes I mainly use cashew butter, almond butter and hazelnut butter. Cashew butter is the most creamy with the most neutral flavour, while almond and hazelnut butters not only add texture to cakes, but great flavour too. I always keep the skins on the almonds and hazelnuts as I like their flavour but you can remove them if you prefer. Almond skins can be removed easily after soaking, but hazelnuts need toasting to remove the skins.

When eaten alone, on tea loaves (see Chapter 2, page 62) or drizzled over porridge, feel free to mix in a little natural liquid sweetener if you want, but do try them without. The taste of the raw nuts, especially when 'activated dried' (see page 25), is just fantastic as it is. I do not use sweetened nut butters in my cakes, as sweeteners are added in the recipes.

I recommend soaking (activating) and drying your nuts (see page 25) when you make nut butters as they taste great and they're better for you, too. But if you do not have time to make your own, then use smooth, unsweetened versions, activated and organic when possible.

## ALMOND, HAZELNUT AND CASHEW NUT BUTTERS

*This method for making smooth nut butter works for any nut, so have a go with your favourite nut or try out different combinations of nuts.*

**Makes 350 g (12¼ oz/1⅓ cups) smooth nut butter**
350 g (12¼ oz / about 2½ cups depending on the type of nut) whole hazelnuts, almonds or cashew nuts, preferably activated dried (see page 25)
Pinch–¼ tsp Himalayan pink salt

Place the nuts in a food processor fitted with a blade and process for 1 minute, gently shaking the machine now and again. Stop, scrape down and process again. Soon, the nuts will start to climb up the edges of the bowl. Continue to process, gently rocking the machine every minute, scraping down when necessary.

After 5–15 minutes, depending on the type of nut, the mixer will start to get a little hot and the ground nuts will start to clump together in balls as a paste forms. Add the salt and continue processing. This is the time to persevere! Keep mixing until really smooth and spreadable. Spoon into a glass jar and store in the fridge for at least one month.

The process will take about 30–40 minutes for harder oilier nuts like almonds, 20–30 minutes for hazelnuts and about 10–15 minutes for softer nuts like cashew nuts.

## TIPS FOR MAKING NUT BUTTERS (ALMOND BUTTER IS SHOWN)

1. It is imperative to use dried nuts, whether 'activated dried' (see page 25) or just from the packet. If the nuts are wet the butter will go off quickly.

2. The whole nuts will soon begin to grind down and the oils in the nuts will help the nut paste to form. Toast the nuts first if you prefer a toasted flavour.

3. Please note all food processors vary in terms of strength and speed. Spoon out the smooth nut butter from the processor into a glass jar.

# Basic Nut Creams

When you start to make these delicious dairy-free nut creams you will realize how amazingly versatile and useful they are either to go with your *Clean Cakes*, or in your day-to-day cooking.

## CASHEW CREAM

*Cashew nuts are a really useful ingredient, especially for those who do not eat dairy, as they can be whizzed up to make silky milks and creams. This unctuous cashew cream is perfect served with any of my* Clean Cakes, *plus it is the base of some icings (frostings), 'yogurts' and raw cakes. It is delicious as it is, or you can adapt it by adding your preferred natural sweetener or other flavourings such as vanilla. I also love to add it to smoothies and stir it into granola, fresh fruit or porridge.*

*For a savoury twist, make a non-dairy soured cream by adding nutritional yeast flakes or powder, lemon juice and salt to taste to the cream. Then stir into soups or enjoy with tacos and chilli.*

**Makes about 380 g (13½ oz/1¾ cups)**
200 g (7 oz / 1½ cups) cashew nuts (about 260 g (9¼ oz) soaked weight)
130 ml (4½ fl oz / generous ½ cup) almond milk (see page 28)

Soak the cashew nuts in 500 ml (17 fl oz / 2⅛ cup) of filtered water and 1 tsp of Himalayan pink salt for 3–4 hours. Drain and rinse thoroughly.

Blend the nuts with the almond milk until completely smooth, stopping the blender and scraping down the mix when necessary. The end result must be totally smooth for use in all recipes.

The cream will keep in the fridge for at least four days in a sealed glass jar.

## WHIPPED COCONUT CREAM

*Serve this dreamily light cream with cakes, fresh fruit or sorbets, or to top warm pancakes and waffles. If you want to make it a little sweeter, add a small amount of clear raw honey or blonde coconut nectar. With their strong and distinctive flavours, date and maple syrup aren't recommended. Vanilla seeds are a perfect addition to this whipped cream, as in my Coconut rose cake on page 48.*

**Makes about 240 g (8½ oz/1¼ cups) whipped coconut cream**
1 x 400 ml (14 fl oz) can of coconut milk

Place the unopened can of coconut milk in the fridge overnight. The next day, open the tin and scrape off the thicker part of the milk, which will have set overnight. You should get about 240 g (8½ oz) of cream. Pour the remaining thinner milk into a glass jar and reserve for later.

Whisk the cream by hand or using a freestanding mixer until soft smooth peaks form, which won't take long.

Once whipped, use immediately or refrigerate. The cream will thicken slightly if kept in the fridge, so stir gently or whip up lightly before use if necessary. You can also add some of the reserved thinner milk to loosen it if you want.

This cream will keep in an airtight container in the fridge for about four to five days. The rest of the reserved coconut milk can be used in smoothies or porridge.

**VARIATION**

***Whipped vanilla coconut cream***
To the above whipped coconut cream, add the seeds from a quarter to half a vanilla pod (bean) – according to your preference and the size of the pod (bean) – and your preferred clear liquid sweetener, to taste, if desired. This goes particularly well with my Chocolate and hazelnut torte with honey praline ganache (see page 39), Hot chocolate chestnut cakes with choco-malt sauce (see page 57), Raspberry and rose tartlets with pistachio frangipane (see page 118) and Baked kabocha squash pie (see page 135).

# Basic Nut Milks

Commercially produced nut milks often contain thickeners and added sweeteners, so I recommend making your own nut milks as not only will they taste better, but you know exactly what is in them. Shop-bought nut milks will work in my recipes, but homemade nut milk's perfect consistency and flavoursome creaminess does make a difference.

If you do not have time to make your own nut milks, homemade almond or cashew milk can be replaced with the shop-bought versions or other neutral-flavoured plant milks such as brown rice or oat milk. Try to source a shop-bought hazelnut milk to replace homemade hazelnut milk, as its distinctive flavour is important in the recipes it's used in. Make sure you select good-quality plant milks, free from additives and sweeteners. See Stockists on page 176.

When making nut milks, a blender works best and gives the best yield. However, you can use a food processor – process the nuts until as small as possible – you will just get a bit less milk and a slightly lumpier pulp. I prefer to strain almond and hazelnut milks so they are smooth, especially for use in my recipes, otherwise you need to compensate for the extra fibre with extra ingredients and flavourings.

If you want a sweeter nut milk, for example to go with granola or porridge, then add your preferred natural sweetener to taste once you have blended the nuts. However, I do not add sweeteners to nut milks used in the recipes in *Clean Cakes*, as sweeteners will be added later. If you want a thinner consistency, for example for using in smoothies, then simply add more water to the milk.

## ALMOND, HAZELNUT, PISTACHIO AND CASHEW NUT MILKS

*I use almond milk in most of my recipes as it is rich and creamy with a subtle flavour, making the perfect canvas onto which other flavours can be carefully and successfully layered. It has wonderful health-boosting properties as it is one of the most beneficial alkaline foods, is high in protein and calcium and contains zinc, vitamin E and essential nutrients for the skin. Cashew milk is a great replacement for almond milk, while hazelnut milk has a slightly stronger flavour. This nut milk recipe can be adapted for most kinds of nuts so play around to find your favourite.*

*Makes 700 ml (24 fl oz/3 cups) almond or hazelnut milk and 200 g (7 oz/compact 1⅛ cups) nut milk pulp / Makes 900 ml (31 fl oz/scant 4 cups) pistachio or cashew milk*

200 g (7 oz/about 1½ cups depending on the type of nut) almonds, hazelnuts, cashew or pistachio nuts
600 ml (21 fl oz/2½ cups) filtered water
Pinch–½ tsp Himalayan pink salt

Soak (activate) the almonds or hazelnuts for 8–12 hours (or overnight), the pistachio nuts for 6–8 hours or the cashew nuts for 3–4 hours in 500 ml (17 fl oz/2⅛ cups) of filtered water with 1 tsp of Himalayan pink salt.

Drain and thoroughly rinse the nuts in a colander or sieve under running water. Place them in a blender with the measured water and your preferred quantity of salt. Blend for about 20 seconds. Stop and repeat until the nuts are well ground and you have a creamy white milk. The pistachio and cashew milks do not need straining.

Fit a nut milk bag or a fine sieve fitted with muslin over a bowl or a jug and pour the almond or hazelnut milk through it. Rinse out the pulp in the blender with 50 ml (1¾ fl oz/scant ¼ cup) of filtered water and add it to the milk. Squeeze the milk through the nut bag until just the pulp remains. You will be left with about 200 g (7 oz/1⅛ cups) of pulp. Do not throw this away as it can be dehydrated (see page 25) and stored in glass jars or used wet as it is in my Waste not, want not multi-seed quinoa bread (see page 87) or Raw herby hemp seed crackers (see page 100).

The nut milks will keep well in the fridge in an airtight glass bottle for about four to five days. If you want to make half a batch then just halve the quantities given above.

## CREAMY SWEET CASHEW MILK

*A smooth and indulgent nut milk, I use this to add creaminess to my recipes and when I need something thicker than my regular nut milk. In raw desserts it makes a great alternative to coconut milk and is delicious warmed up with cacao and a little chilli, cinnamon and cardamom for an extra thick hot chocolate.*

*Makes 280 ml (9½ fl oz/1¼ cups)*
70 g (2½ oz/½ cup) cashew nuts
200 ml (7 fl oz/generous ¾ cup) filtered water
½ tbsp date syrup
Pinch of Himalayan pink salt

Soak the cashew nuts for 3–4 hours in 200 ml (7 fl oz/generous ¾ cup) of filtered water and scant ½ tsp of Himalayan pink salt. Drain and thoroughly rinse the nuts in a sieve or colander under running water. Blend the nuts with the rest of the ingredients in a blender until completely smooth. No straining is required. Store as for nut milks.

# Basic Pastry

Great pastry should be light, crumbly and a little crunchy – and believe me, this can certainly be achieved without using dairy butter! There's no need to worry about chewy overworked pastry any more as the crumb made with gluten-free flour, here a combination of buckwheat flour and ground almonds (almond meal), is perfect, the fat from the coconut oil adding the final necessary flakiness. As you will be filling this pastry with sweet fresh fruits, nuts and chocolate, you don't need too much sweetness in the base.

The number of times I use this pastry as a base in Chapter 4, Gorgeous tarts and scrumptious pies, just proves how great it is. So, after making it a few times, following my recipes, why not have a go at thinking up your own tasty fillings. Or try replacing the ground almonds (almond meal) with other ground nuts, as I do in my Pear, chocolate and hazelnut tart with cacao pastry crust (see page 121); a pecan crust with an apple and blackberry filling; a pistachio crust with a raspberry jam (jelly) (see page 32) and dark (bittersweet) chocolate ganache (see page 160) filling; the possibilities are endless.

For savoury ideas see my Tomato and pepper pissaladière on page 126 and my Roasted root vegetable tarts on page 125.

After lining your tart shells any leftover pastry can be baked off as biscuits (cookies) or frozen.

*Makes 550 g (1 lb 3 oz) pastry, enough to line two 23 cm (9 inch) round tart tins*

150 g (5¼ oz / 1 cup) buckwheat flour
150 g (5¼ oz / 1¼ cups) ground almonds (almond meal)
60 g (2 oz / ½ cup) coconut sugar
20 g (¾ oz / 2½ tbsp) arrowroot
½ tsp Himalayan pink salt
Finely grated zest of 1 lemon
100 g (3½ oz / ½ cup) coconut oil, plus extra for greasing
70 ml (2½ fl oz / ¼ cup plus 2 tsp) cool water

I use a freestanding mixer with a paddle attachment to make this pastry, but you can use a mixing bowl with a wooden spoon or spatula if preferred.

## MAKING THE PASTRY

1. Grease your tins with coconut oil. Combine all the dry ingredients, including the lemon zest. A whisk is good for this as it gets rid of any lumps.

2. Melt the coconut oil and gradually pour it into the dry ingredients, followed by the water, mixing until everything is well combined. At this point the dough can be wrapped in baking parchment and then cling film (plastic wrap) and frozen for up to one month or kept in the fridge for about five days.

## LINING YOUR TART TIN

3. Divide the dough in two. On lightly floured baking parchment, flatten the dough with your hands to a round shape, about 1 cm (⅓ inch) thick. Lightly flour the pastry, cover with baking parchment and roll out evenly with a rolling pin to 3 mm (⅛ inch) thick. Repeat with the rest of the dough. Refrigerate on a flat tray for 10 minutes.

4. Remove the pastry from the fridge, take off the top layer of parchment, then flip the pastry over onto the tin, peeling off the second layer of parchment. Press the dough gently into the tin. Fix any holes, making sure there are no gaps. The lined tins will keep in the fridge for up to five days or you can freeze them for at least a month.

## BLIND BAKING

5. 'Blind baking' is the process of partly or fully baking a pastry shell before it is filled. To do this, after lining the prepared tin with the pastry, place a layer of baking parchment over the chilled pastry. Fill the pastry with baking beans or dried rice and bake at 170°C/325°F/Gas Mark 3 according to the recipe's timings.

6. Remove the baking beans or rice and baking parchment, bake for about 10 minutes longer or until a light golden colour, then continue as instructed in the recipe.

# Jams (Jellies) and Apple Purée

*No more slaving away over a hot stove! Natural sweeteners make these fresh-flavoured jams (jellies) and apple purée.*

## QUICK-COOK RASPBERRY JAM (JELLY)

The recipe for my Quick-blend raw raspberry chia jam (jelly) (see below) is great for a quick and easy jam (jelly), but sometimes a sweeter, more traditional version is necessary. This is so full of flavour only small amounts are needed. Perfectly tart and sweet at the same time, it adds the ideal fruity oomph to my Dark (bittersweet) chocolate dipped peanut butter and jelly dreams (see page 94).

*Makes about 200 g (7 oz/¾ cup)*
200 g (7 oz/1½ cups) raspberries, fresh or frozen
100 g (3½ oz/⅓ cup plus 1 tbsp) no-added-sugar grape
    concentrate
50 g (1¾ oz/2 tbsp) date syrup

Warm a small–medium sterilized jam (jelly) jar (holding 200 ml (7 fl oz/¾ cup) in an oven no hotter than 100°C/210°F/Gas Mark ¼. Put a saucer or small plate in the fridge.

Place all the ingredients in a small–medium saucepan and bring to the boil. Boil for about 3 minutes, then turn down to a low simmer for a further 5 minutes, stirring occasionally. By this point, a lot of the liquid will have evaporated. Stir continuously for about 5 more minutes, being careful not to let it catch on the pan. By now you should have a perfectly thick and sticky jam (jelly), but still slightly runny. If it is overcooked, it will set too hard.

To check it is ready, place a teaspoon of the jam (jelly) on the chilled saucer and return to the fridge for a few minutes. It is ready when the cooled tester has formed a slight skin, which will wrinkle when pushed. If the jam (jelly) isn't ready, cook for a few more minutes and test again.

Pour into the warmed sterilized jar, cover with a circle of wax paper (or baking parchment), and seal with a lid. Lasts up to three months in the fridge.

## QUICK-BLEND RAW RASPBERRY CHIA JAM (JELLY)

This is a really useful recipe for an instant jam (jelly) fix and works well in raw desserts and mixed with my 'yogurts'. It has a wonderfully fresh flavour, with the dates helping to thicken and add sweetness while the chia seeds provide extra binding. This jam (jelly) works particularly well with raspberries, strawberries or plums. Try making it with your favourite fruit, considering tartness and sweetness, and add more dates or lemon juice if necessary.

*Makes about 300 g (10½ oz/1¼ cups)*
100 g (3½ oz/⅔ cup) pitted Medjool dates, finely chopped
200 g (7 oz/1½ cups) raspberries, preferably fresh but you
    can use just defrosted frozen
½ tbsp chia seeds
½ tsp lemon juice, optional

Blend the dates and 150 g (5¼ oz/1⅛ cup) of raspberries until smooth, using a hand-held or freestanding blender. Stop the blender and scrape down a few times if necessary. Remove from the blender and add the rest of the raspberries, crushing them with a fork, to add texture. Then add the chia seeds. Leave to thicken, stirring occasionally, for 15 minutes. Taste and add lemon juice if desired. Will keep in an airtight glass jar in the fridge for about five days.

*Notes: If you don't have Medjool dates, use sweet pitted dates; if dry, soak in warm water for 30 minutes, then finely chop.*
*If you want to halve this recipe, make it by hand as the quantity will not be large enough to hit the blender blades. Chop the dates (the softer, the better) and make into a smooth paste with the back of a knife, then add the fruit and chia seeds last.*

## EASY APPLE PURÉE

*Quick and extremely simple to make – no peeling or coring is required – the end product is a great addition to a Clean Cakes kitchen. Apple purée not only adds a natural low-GI fibre-full sweetener to your cakes, it also adds moisture and helps create a wonderfully soft texture. Any well-flavoured sweet apples will work, but cooking times vary with different apples, so keep an eye on them. Decrease or increase the amount as you wish.*

*Makes about 1 kg (2 lb 3 oz/4 cups)*
12 apples (each 120–140 g/4¼–5 oz), I like Cox's

Preheat the oven to 180°C/350°F/Gas Mark 4. Wash and dry the apples then cut into quarters. Place on a baking tray and bake until soft, about 20–30 minutes. Leave to cool and do not discard the liquids. In a blender, blend the cooked apples and juices until a smooth, sweet, thick purée.

Either use immediately, keep in the fridge for up to five days or freeze in batches in glass jars.

# All the cakes

# Courgette (zucchini), basil, lime and pistachio cake with avocado lime cream and raspberry jam (jelly)

*Serves 12*

**Courgette (zucchini) cake**

90 g (3 oz / ⅔ cup) pistachio nuts, preferably activated dried (see page 25)

60 g (2 oz / ½ cup) coconut flour

1½ tsp baking powder

1½ tsp bicarbonate of soda (baking soda)

180 g (6¼ oz) courgettes (zucchini), grated

150 g (5¼ oz / scant ⅔ cup) natural coconut yogurt

150 g (5¼ oz / scant 1¼ cups) coconut sugar

3 eggs

¼ tsp Himalayan pink salt

Finely grated zest of 3 limes

15 g (½ oz / ½ cup) basil leaves, finely chopped, plus about 4 extra leaves for scattering over the lime cream

60 g (2 oz / generous ¼ cup) coconut oil, melted, plus extra for greasing

**Avocado lime cream**

200 g (7 oz) avocado flesh (about 1 large avocado)

250 g (8¾ oz / 1 cup) natural coconut yogurt

100 g (3½ oz / scant ½ cup) blonde coconut nectar

Finely grated zest of 1½ limes

60 ml (2 fl oz / ¼ cup) lime juice

80 g (2¾ oz / ⅓ cup plus 1 tbsp) coconut oil, melted

**To finish**

170 g (6 oz / scant ¾ cup) quick-cook raspberry jam (jelly) (see page 32) or no added sugar high fruit content raspberry jam (jelly)

Small handful chopped pistachio nuts

Edible flowers such as honeysuckle or rose

*This cake sings with fresh summer flavours. The courgette (zucchini) keeps the sponge layers wonderfully soft as they ooze with the refreshingly light lime cream and sharp raspberry jam (jelly). I love to finish it with edible flowers from my garden. It makes a show-stopping birthday cake, too.*

Make the avocado lime cream first as it needs time to firm up in the fridge. Blend the avocado, coconut yogurt, coconut nectar, lime zest and juice in a blender until smooth. Add the coconut oil and blend until completely smooth. Place in a bowl and cover the surface of the cream completely with cling film (plastic wrap) so it does not oxidize and lose its colour. Chill in the fridge for 2–3 hours to firm up.

Preheat the oven to 170°C / 325°F / Gas Mark 3. Grease and line the base of three 23 cm (9 inch) loose-bottomed or springform cake tins with coconut oil and baking parchment. Line a small baking tray with baking parchment.

Spread the pistachio nuts out on the lined baking tray and toast for 5–7 minutes until just getting colour. Leave to cool then roughly chop into small pieces.

Sieve together the coconut flour, baking powder and bicarbonate of soda (baking soda) into a bowl. In a large bowl, mix together the rest of the sponge ingredients except for the oil. Add in the sieved flour mix and chopped nuts, then finally stir in the oil. Divide the mix equally between the three tins (about 300 g (10½ oz) per tin). Spread the mix with a palette knife (frosting spatula) or small knife to make a thin layer.

Bake for 10 minutes, rotate the tins and bake for another 10 minutes until the top is dark golden brown and bounces back slightly when pressed. Leave to cool, remove from the tins and carefully peel off the baking parchment from the bottom of each sponge.

To assemble, spread the bottom layer of the sponge with half the jam (jelly) and about a quarter of the avocado lime cream. Tear the basil leaves into small pieces and scatter half over the lime cream. Top with the middle layer of sponge and repeat the process with the jam (jelly), cream and basil. Carefully place on the final layer of sponge and top with the remaining cream, spreading it over the top of the cake and around the edges. Decorate with chopped pistachio nuts and edible flowers.

This cake will keep in the fridge for up to three days but it is best eaten fresh when all the flavours and colours are at their most vibrant.

**VARIATION**

*Lime mousse*

Serve the Avocado lime cream in small glasses or cups, topped with shavings of fresh coconut, to make a light and fresh end to a meal.

# Chocolate and hazelnut torte with honey praline ganache

*Serves 10–12*

**Praline paste**

90 g (3 oz / generous ⅓ cup) hazelnut butter (see page 26)

90 g (3 oz / generous ⅓ cup) almond butter (see page 26)

20 g (¾ oz / 1 tbsp) raw honey

20 g (¾ oz / 2 tbsp) Palmyra nectar powder

¼ tsp Himalayan pink salt

**Chocolate and hazelnut torte**

160 g (5½ oz / 1⅛ cup) hazelnuts, preferably activated dried (see page 25)

100 g (3½ oz) homemade chocolate (see page 156) or dark (bittersweet) chocolate 85% cocoa solids

100 g (3½ oz / ½ cup) coconut oil

100 g (3½ oz / ⅓ cup) praline paste (see above)

3 eggs, separated

½ tsp Himalayan pink salt

2 tsp vanilla extract

50 g (1¾ oz / ⅓ cup) Palmyra nectar powder

**Honey praline ganache**

90 g (3 oz) homemade chocolate (see page 156) or dark (bittersweet) chocolate 85% cocoa solids

120 g (4¼ oz) (the rest of the) praline paste (see above)

100 ml (3½ fl oz / ⅓ cup plus 1 tbsp) hazelnut milk (see page 28)

35 g (1¼ oz / scant 2 tbsp) raw honey

*A chocoholic's delight! Instead of using shop-bought praline or chocolate and hazelnut spread, both packed with refined sugar, I make my own praline paste using nut butters and natural sweeteners. It adds a really pure nutty flavour and texture to this rich and decadent cake without making it sickly sweet.*

Preheat the oven to 170°C / 325°F / Gas Mark 3. Grease and line the bottom of a 23 cm (9 inch) springform cake tin with coconut oil.

To make the homemade praline paste, mix everything together well and set aside.

To make the torte, line a baking tray and toast the hazelnuts for about 7 minutes. Set aside 60 g (2 oz / scant ½ cup) of the hazelnuts for the topping. Remove the skins from the remaining hazelnuts and blitz in a food processor until as fine as possible.

Slowly melt the chocolate over a bain-marie (see page 156) then add the coconut oil. When everything has melted, remove from the heat and add the measured praline paste. Stir to combine. Add the ground nuts, egg yolks, half the salt and the vanilla extract to the chocolate mix.

Whip the egg whites with the remaining salt until fully whipped and firm, add the Palmyra nectar powder and whip a little more to combine. You should have soft caramel-coloured peaks. Very gently fold the egg whites into the chocolate mix, about a third at a time. Mix until just combined and do not overmix – it should look like a light chocolate mousse.

Pour into the prepared tin and bake for 10 minutes, rotate and bake for another 5 minutes. A skewer inserted in the centre should come out clean, the top should be light but firm to touch, and you should hear air bubbles popping when you touch it. Leave to cool in the tin then demould.

To make the ganache, melt the chocolate over a bain-marie (see page 156). Take off the heat and stir in the praline paste. In a small saucepan, warm the hazelnut milk with the honey. When it is warm and the honey has dissolved, gradually pour it over the chocolate, stirring continuously until a thick and glossy emulsion forms. Cover the surface with baking parchment and leave in a cool place for about 1 hour until the cake has completely cooled and the ganache has thickened. Stir the ganache lightly and spread it over the cooled cake using a palette knife (frosting spatula). For a firmer set ganache, just leave it for a little longer. Chop the remaining hazelnuts in half, scatter them over the ganache and serve.

This torte is lovely with whipped vanilla coconut cream (see page 27) and keeps for up to five days in the fridge. It freezes well too, with the ganache on top!

# Clementine and pomegranate jewel cake

..................................................................................................................

*Make this stunning cake during the winter months when clementines are at their sweetest and best. It is a light and fresh alternative to the heavier food around at this time of year. When serving this cake, I like to cut open an extra pomegranate for its seeds, so that each slice is served with a generous amount of pomegranate 'jewels'.*

..................................................................................................................

*Serves 8–10*

**Clementine cake**

450 g (1 lb) clementines (about 5)

4 eggs

150 g (5¼ oz / scant 1¼ cups) coconut sugar

225 g (8 oz / 2 cups) ground almonds (almond meal)

1 tsp baking powder

**Pomegranate jewel syrup**

120 ml (4 fl oz / ½ cup) 100% pomegranate juice, not from concentrate

30 g (1 oz / 1½ tbsp) raw honey

1 tbsp pomegranate molasses

1 large pomegranate, about 450 g (1 lb), plus extra seeds for serving

Cook the clementines by placing them in a lidded saucepan with cold water to cover. Bring to the boil, turn down to a low heat and simmer for 2 hours, topping up the water when necessary, until the fruit is soft and a skewer pierces it easily. Drain and leave to cool.

Preheat the oven to 180°C / 350°F / Gas Mark 4. Grease the bottom and sides of a 23 cm (9 inch) springform 'crown' cake tin. Line the base with baking parchment.

Cut the cooled clementines in half, remove any pips and then blitz the whole fruits, including the skin, in a food processor until a smooth pulp forms.

Whisk the eggs and sugar together, then mix in the ground almonds (almond meal) and baking powder with a wooden spoon or spatula. Then add the clementine pulp to the rest of the ingredients, folding lightly in until well combined.

Pour into the tin and bake for 20 minutes, rotate the tin and bake for a further 20 minutes or until a skewer inserted into the centre of the cake comes out clean. If the top is looking a bit too brown, reduce the temperature to 170°C / 325°F / Gas Mark 3 for the last 10 minutes of baking. Remove from the oven and leave to cool completely in the tin.

To make the pomegranate jewel syrup, in a saucepan bring the pomegranate juice, honey and pomegranate molasses to a boil, turn down the heat and simmer for 5 minutes. Remove from the heat then break open the pomegranate over the saucepan, letting the seeds and juices fall into the syrup. Stir well.

When the cake has cooled, remove it from the tin and transfer to a serving plate. Pour over the syrup and seeds, letting them fall into the middle of the cake, then slice and serve with extra pomegranate seeds. Keeps for up to five days in a sealed container, preferably in the fridge. It freezes well too.

**NOTES**

*If you don't have a springform 'crown' cake tin you can make this in any 20–23 cm (8–9 inch) regular round springform cake tin.*

*Pomegranate molasses is made from the concentrated juice of pomegranates and has a brown-red hue. It is packed with vitamins, minerals and antioxidants and has a tangy and slightly bitter flavour. Mixed with a little honey it makes a sweet and fruity glaze or syrup for cakes as shown here, especially complementing citrus.*

# Pumpkin, carrot and walnut cake with cashew orange 'frosting'

*Serves 8–12*

**Pumpkin cake**

90 g (3 oz / generous ¾ cup) walnuts, preferably activated dried (see page 25)

70 g (2½ oz / ½ cup) teff flour

70 g (2½ oz / ½ cup) brown rice flour

15 g (½ oz / 2 tbsp) arrowroot

¾ tsp Himalayan pink salt

1 tsp bicarbonate of soda (baking soda)

1½ tsp mixed spice

1½ tsp ground cinnamon

120 g (4¼ oz / generous ¾ cup) Palmyra nectar powder

60 g (2 oz / generous ⅓ cup) sultanas (seedless golden raisins)

150 ml (5 fl oz / scant ⅔ cup) EVCP rapeseed oil, plus extra for greasing

210 g (7½ oz / scant 1 cup) good-quality tinned pumpkin purée (or homemade)

60 g (2 oz / ⅔ cup) grated carrot

Finely grated zest of 1 orange

2 eggs

**Cashew orange 'frosting'**

1 x recipe cashew cream (see page 27)

80 g (2¾ oz / ¼ cup) clear raw honey

¼ vanilla pod (bean), split lengthways and seeds scraped out

Finely grated zest and 4 tsp juice of ½ lemon

Finely grated zest of 1 orange

Pinch Himalayan pink salt

140 g (5 oz / ⅔ cup) coconut oil, melted

**To decorate**

Edible flowers, such as fresh and dried marigolds

*This is similar to a carrot cake, but so much better! With its spices and distinctive deep flavours of the teff flour, Palmyra nectar and the nutty cold pressed rapeseed oil, it's a delightfully warming cake. The pumpkin purée keeps it scrumptiously soft while studded with lightly toasted crunchy walnuts and juicy sultanas (seedless golden raisins).*

Make the frosting first as it needs time in the fridge to firm up. To make the frosting, combine all the ingredients except the coconut oil in a blender, finishing by blending in the oil. Blend until totally smooth, cover the surface completely with cling film (plastic wrap) and refrigerate for about 8 hours or ideally overnight to thicken.

Preheat the oven to 170°C / 325°F / Gas Mark 3. On a baking tray, lightly toast the walnuts for 5–8 minutes, until just beginning to colour, leave to cool then chop into small pea-sized pieces. Grease an 18–20 cm (7–8 inch) loose-bottomed cake tin with rapeseed oil and line the base with baking parchment.

In a large bowl, mix together the walnuts with all the dry ingredients from the teff flour to the sultanas (seedless golden raisins). In another bowl, mix together the oil, pumpkin purée, grated carrot, orange zest and eggs. Make a well in the centre of the dry ingredients and pour in the wet ingredients, folding them in until combined.

Pour the mix into the prepared tin and bake for 30–35 minutes, rotating halfway through baking, or until a skewer inserted in the centre comes out clean. Leave to cool in the tin and then demould. When cool, cut in half and fill with half the cashew orange 'frosting', spreading the remainder on top. If your frosting is a little too runny and needs to be firmer, give it a blast in the freezer for about 10 minutes. Decorate with fresh flowers, if you wish.

This keeps well for up to five days in the fridge. It freezes well too, without the frosting.

### NOTES

*You can also make muffins with the cake mix. Just divide the mix between eight muffin cases and bake at 170°C/325°F/Gas Mark 3 for 15–20 minutes, turning halfway, until a skewer inserted into the centre of a muffin comes out clean. Top with the frosting, or they're delicious without.*

*Pecans work well instead of walnuts in this cake.*

# Pear, honey and walnut upside-down cake

**Serves 10–12**

70 g (2½ oz / ⅔ cup) walnuts, preferably activated dried (see page 25)

180 g (6¼ oz / generous ½ cup) raw honey

4–5 medium to large pears (about 800 g (1 lb 12 oz))

120 g (4¼ oz / generous ½ cup) non-hydrogenated dairy-free butter, plus extra for greasing

80 g (2¾ oz / ½ cup) Palmyra nectar powder

80 g (2¾ oz / ⅓ cup) easy apple purée (see page 32)

½ tsp vanilla extract

60 g (2 oz / ⅓ cup plus 1 tbsp) brown rice flour

60 g (2 oz / ⅓ cup plus 1 tbsp) teff flour

20 g (¾ oz / 2½ tbsp) arrowroot

½ tsp baking powder

½ tsp bicarbonate of soda (baking soda)

¼ tsp xanthan gum

½ tsp Himalayan pink salt

2 eggs

*Nourishing teff and brown rice flours with Palmyra nectar prove yet again to be a winning combination in this cake, brimming with goodness and scrumptiousness. Fragrant local honey and sweet pear juices seep into the light walnut sponge, making it satisfyingly soft. This is one of my favourite autumn-winter bakes.*

Preheat the oven to 170°C / 325°F / Gas Mark 3. Grease a 23 cm (9 inch) springform cake tin with butter and line the bottom with baking parchment; make the circle of parchment on the bottom of the tin come up the edges of the tin by 2 cm (¾ inch) to stop the juices and honey seeping out.

Line a baking tray with baking parchment. Spread the walnuts out on the lined baking tray and lightly toast for 5–8 minutes until just beginning to colour. Leave to cool and then chop finely to very small pieces.

Spoon the honey evenly into the base of the tin. Peel, quarter, core and slice the pears to 1 cm (⅓ inch) thick slices (you should have about 450–500 g (1lb–1 lb 2 oz) of slices). Arrange the slices in the tin in a circle like rays of sun, overlapping them, starting from the centre then working out.

Using a handheld whisk or freestanding mixer, whisk the butter, Palmyra nectar powder, apple purée and vanilla extract until soft, smooth and light caramel in colour. Combine the flours, arrowroot, baking powder, bicarbonate of soda (baking soda), xanthan gum and salt. If using a mixer, change the whisk to a paddle, and add the dry ingredients to the butter mixture, alternating with the eggs; or mix in by hand. Finally add the chopped walnuts and mix until just combined. Pour the mix over the sliced pears, smooth it out if necessary, and bake for 20 minutes. Rotate the tin and bake for a further 10–15 minutes, until the top is dark golden brown and a skewer inserted in the centre of the sponge comes out clean.

Leave to cool on a wire rack for about 30 minutes, then remove from the tin (it is easier to remove while still warm) and invert onto a plate. Serve warm with a cup of tea, or it makes a divine pudding with vanilla cashew 'yogurt' (see page 53) or vanilla ice cream. Keeps well for at least three days in a sealed container.

**VARIATIONS**

*Quince, honey and walnut upside-down cake*
Follow the recipe above, replacing the pears with 3 medium quinces, peeled, cored and quartered and cut into ½ cm (⅕ inch) slices.

*Spiced pineapple upside-down cake*
Follow the recipe above, replacing the pears with about three-quarters of a pineapple and the walnuts with the same amount of pecan nuts. Add 5 g (⅕ oz / 1 tbsp) finely chopped fresh ginger and half a finely chopped small red chilli to the honey in the base of the tin. Peel the pineapple and slice into six 1.5 cm (½ inch) rings, removing the hard centres. Add 10 g (⅓ oz / 2 tbsp) more finely chopped ginger and the finely grated zest of 1 lime to the cake mix. Cover the honey, ginger and chilli mixture with the pineapple, top with the ginger and lime cake mix and bake as above.

# Blackberry and apple cinnamon crumble cake

*Serves 8–10*

120 g (4¼ oz / 1⅛ cups) walnuts,
  preferably activated dried (see
  page 25)
1 tbsp milled flax seeds
3 tbsp filtered water
100 g (3½ oz / 1 cup less 2 tbsp) ground
  almonds (almond meal)
70 g (2½ oz / ½ cup) chestnut flour
1 tsp ground cinnamon
1 tsp baking powder
1 tsp bicarbonate of soda (baking soda)
½ tsp Himalayan pink salt
Zest of ½ lemon
60 g (2 oz / ¼ cup) easy apple purée
  (see page 32)
80 g (2¾ oz / ¼ cup) maple syrup
1 tsp vanilla extract
50 ml (1¾ fl oz / scant ¼ cup) EVCP
  rapeseed oil, plus extra for greasing
2 dessert apples such as Cox or Granny
  Smith (250–300 g (8¾–10½ oz) total
  weight)
250 g (8¾ oz / 2½ cups) blackberries,
  fresh or frozen

*I love slicing this cake in front of friends, each piece revealing the white apple slices dyed by the purple blackberry juices, listening to the satisfied 'oohs' and 'aahs' as people delve into the three layers of crunchy crumble topping, sweet fruit and deliciously gooey cake. It is warming, comforting, autumnal wholefood at its best.*

Preheat the oven to 170°C / 325°F / Gas Mark 3. Line the bottom of an 18–20 cm (7–8 inch) loose-bottomed cake tin with baking parchment and grease the sides with a little oil. Place the walnuts on a baking tray and toast in the oven for 5–8 minutes until beginning to colour. Leave to cool. Finely chop 80 g (2¾ oz / ¾ cup) and set aside the remaining walnuts.

Combine the milled flax seeds with the water and leave for 15 minutes to form a gel, stirring occasionally. In a large bowl, mix together the finely chopped walnuts, ground almonds (almond meal), chestnut flour, cinnamon, baking powder, bicarbonate of soda (baking soda), salt and lemon zest. Make a well in the centre and add the flax gel, apple purée, maple syrup, vanilla extract and oil and mix to combine.

Divide the mix equally in two, place half the mix in the cake tin and spread it out with a palette knife (frosting spatula). It should be about 1 cm (⅓ inch) deep and weigh about 250 g (8¾ oz). Peel, core and thinly slice the apples. Spread them over the cake mix, overlapping them in a circle, followed by the blackberries and top with the rest of the cake mix. The mix will be sticky so use your fingers to dab small bits of the mix over the blackberries. It doesn't matter if some berries are still showing, but try to cover most of them.

Sprinkle the remaining walnuts over the top of the cake, breaking them up roughly between your fingers as you do so. Press them into the cake mix slightly. Bake for about 30 minutes, rotating the tin halfway through baking. It is ready when the top is firm to touch and a rich golden brown, the nuts will be well toasted and a skewer inserted into the centre of the cake comes out almost clean. If the top is looking a bit too dark, turn down the oven to 160°C / 310°F / Gas Mark 2½ for the last 10–15 minutes.

Serve warm with an extra dusting of cinnamon or mesquite (see page 54) if you like and natural yogurt. This is best easten fresh but will keep for up to five days in a sealed container in the fridge.

*NOTE*
*Sliced pears make good replacements for the apple.*

# Coconut rose cake with whipped vanilla coconut cream

*Serves 10–12*

### Coconut rose cake

Coconut oil, for greasing

Gluten-free flour, such as brown rice flour, for dusting

5 eggs, separated

150 g (5¼ oz / scant 1¼ cups) coconut sugar

100 g (3½ oz / 1¼ cups) desiccated coconut

2 tbsp plus ½ tsp rosewater

¼ tsp Himalayan pink salt

### Vanilla coconut cream

1 vanilla pod (bean), split lengthways and seeds scraped out

50 g (1¾ oz / 2½ tbsp) raw clear honey or blonde coconut nectar

2 x recipe whipped coconut cream (see page 27), about 480 g (1 lb 1 oz)

### To decorate

½–1 tbsp rosewater, for dabbing

100 g (3½ oz / 1⅓ cups) toasted flaked coconut

*Fragrant rosewater subtly infuses this sumptuous Middle Eastern-inspired cake. The alternating layers of delicate thin sponge with the unctuous whipped coconut cream create an exquisitely light cake. Shaved fresh coconut or toasted flaked coconut makes the perfect final touch.*

Preheat the oven to 190°C/375°F/Gas Mark 5. Line the bottom of an 18 cm (7 inch) loose-bottomed cake tin with greaseproof (wax) paper, then grease the edges with coconut oil and lightly flour with gluten-free flour.

In a large bowl, beat the egg yolks with half of the coconut sugar and the desiccated coconut and rosewater. In a freestanding mixer or with a handheld whisk, whip the egg whites with the salt until firm and fluffy then whisk in the remaining coconut sugar. Very gently fold in the egg whites to the yolk and coconut mixture, about a third at a time, making sure to mix very lightly until just combined.

Pour into the cake tin and bake for 20 minutes, rotate the tin and bake for a further 15 minutes, or until the top is dark golden brown, bounces back when you touch it, and a skewer inserted into the centre of the cake comes out clean. The dark brown colour of the cake is normal. Leave to cool.

Make the vanilla coconut cream by folding the vanilla seeds and honey or coconut nectar into the whipped coconut cream. Divide roughly into four.

When the cake has cooled, carefully cut it into three layers using a large serrated knife. The bottom layer might look a little wet, but do not worry. Dab each layer with a little rosewater, using ½–1 tbsp in total. Sandwich together the layers of sponge, using a palette knife (frosting spatula) to spread a quarter of the cream onto each layer, including the top of the cake. The final quarter of cream should be carefully spread around the edges of the cake so the whole cake is encased in the cream.

To finish, cover the whole cake with the toasted flaked coconut and serve. Keeps for at least three days in the fridge.

# Torta di riso with cinnamon saffron almond milk

......................................................................................................

*When I was 20, I lived in Bologna in Italy for five months. It was a truly unforgettable experience and I loved immersing myself in Italian culture, especially the food – I could not walk past a 'pasticceria' without going in. Torta di riso was something I had never seen nor tasted before, a bit like rice pudding in cake-form, but so much more.*

......................................................................................................

*Serves 10–12*

**Torta di riso**

200 g (7 oz / generous 1 cup) short-grain brown rice

400 ml (14 fl oz / scant 1¾ cups) filtered water

60 g (2 oz / generous ⅓ cup) sultanas (seedless golden raisins)

40 ml (1½ fl oz / 8 tsp) rum, optional, or 40 ml (1½ fl oz / 8 tsp) black tea

500 ml (17 fl oz / 2⅛ cup) almond milk (see page 28)

1 cinnamon stick, 8 cm (3 inch) length

1 vanilla pod (bean), split lengthways and seeds scraped out, pod (bean) kept

130 g (4½ oz / generous 1 cup) coconut sugar

3 eggs

60 g (2 oz / scant ½ cup) pine nuts

Finely grated zest of 1 lemon

½ tsp ground cinnamon

½ tsp Himalayan pink salt

75 g (2¾ oz / ⅓ cup) coconut butter or non-hydrogenated dairy-free butter, plus extra for greasing

**Cinnamon saffron almond milk**

200 ml (7 fl oz / ¾ cup plus 1 tbsp) almond milk (see page 28)

3–4 small saffron strands

2 tsp raw honey

Pinch ground cinnamon, adjust to taste

Soak the brown rice in 500 ml (17 fl oz / 2⅛ cup) of filtered water with 1 tsp of lemon juice or apple cider vinegar for 8–12 hours or overnight, then drain and rinse well.

Preheat the oven to 160°C / 310°F / Gas Mark 2½ and grease and line the base and sides of a 23 cm (9 inch) springform cake tin with baking parchment.

In a medium–large saucepan, cover the rice with the measured water, bring to the boil and simmer until the water has been completely absorbed, stirring the rice now and again to stop it from catching, but do not agitate it too much. Soak the sultanas (seedless golden raisins) in the rum, or black tea, to cover, and set aside.

When all the water has been absorbed by the rice, add 250 ml (8½ fl oz / 1 cup) of the almond milk with the cinnamon stick, the vanilla seeds and pod (bean) and 40 g (1½ oz / ⅓ cup) of the coconut sugar. Boil for about 10 more minutes, stirring occasionally, then add the remaining almond milk and continue to cook and stir. The whole process of cooking the rice will take about 30 minutes. The cooked rice should be soft with a little chew and nearly all of the milk should have been absorbed. When it is at this stage, remove from the heat and set aside. Remove the cinnamon stick and empty vanilla pod (bean) and discard.

In a large bowl, whisk together the remaining sugar with the eggs, half the pine nuts, the lemon zest, cinnamon, salt, sultanas (seedless golden raisins) and rum (or tea). Melt the butter and stir in. Finally mix in the slightly cooled rice, stirring to disperse any lumps. Pour the mix into the prepared tin, top with the remaining pine nuts and bake for 30–40 minutes, rotating the cake halfway, until the top is dark golden brown and the cake is firm to touch and when pressed lightly bounces back.

To make the saffron milk, warm all the ingredients in a saucepan until it just comes to a boil. Remove from the heat immediately and add extra cinnamon to taste if you wish.

Leave the cake to cool in the tin on a wire rack and serve at room temperature, on its own, or with the warm cinnamon saffron milk. It is ideal for breakfast or at tea time. This is best kept in the fridge, where it will keep well for at least five days.

*NOTE*

*I recommend making homemade almond milk (see page 28) for this recipe as its depth of flavour really enhances this cake.*

# Rhubarb and orange polenta (cornmeal) cupcakes with strawberry orange blossom compote

*Makes 15 small cakes*

**Rhubarb cupcakes**

1 tbsp milled flax seeds
3 tbsp filtered water
½ tsp apple cider vinegar
120 ml (4 fl oz / ½ cup) almond milk
  (see page 28)
300 g (10½ oz) rhubarb
Finely grated zest of 1 orange
140 g (5 oz / ⅔ cup) coconut nectar
1 tsp vanilla extract
100 g (3½ oz / scant ⅔ cup) fine polenta
  (cornmeal)
100 g (3½ oz / ⅔ cup) brown rice flour
4 tsp arrowroot
1 tsp bicarbonate of soda (baking soda)
½ tsp baking powder
½ tsp Himalayan pink salt
60 g (2 oz / generous ¼ cup) coconut oil,
  melted

**Strawberry compote**

200 g (7 oz) rhubarb
1 vanilla pod (bean), cut in half
  lengthways and seeds scraped out
1–2 tbsp raw honey or coconut nectar
4 oranges
300 g (10½ oz) strawberries, cut into
  quarters
3 tsp orange blossom water

**Vanilla cashew 'yogurt'**

1 x recipe cashew cream (see page 27)
½ vanilla pod (bean), cut in half
  lengthways and seeds scraped out
Finely grated zest and 4 tsp juice of ½
  lemon
40 g (1½ oz / 2 tbsp) raw clear honey or
  blonde coconut nectar
1½ tsp vanilla extract

*Delightfully soft and crumbly, these vegan cakes have a subtle sweet sharpness from the rhubarb. Served with the orange blossom-scented compote and the creamy 'yogurt', this makes for a beautifully coloured sublime spring-summer pudding.*

Preheat the oven to 170°C / 325°F / Gas Mark 3 and line 15 small cake tins or muffin moulds with cake cases.

Combine the milled flax seeds with the water to form a gel, leaving to soak for 15 minutes. Stir the vinegar into the almond milk and set aside. Chop the rhubarb into ½ cm (⅕ inch) slices. In a bowl, combine it with the orange zest, coconut nectar and vanilla extract.

In a large bowl, combine all the dry ingredients from the polenta (cornmeal) to the salt. Make a well in the centre of the dry ingredients and mix in the flax seed gel, almond milk mix, coconut oil and rhubarb, along with its juices, until just combined. Spoon the mix equally between the cake cases and bake for 10 minutes, then reduce the heat to 160°C / 310°F / Gas Mark 2½ and bake for a further 10 minutes, until the tops are golden brown and firm to touch and a skewer inserted into a cake comes out clean. Leave to cool.

To make the compote, wash and dry the rhubarb, trim off the tops and ends and cut diagonally into 2.5 cm (1 inch) pieces. Put on a baking tray with half the vanilla seeds and the empty vanilla pod (bean), 1 tbsp of honey or coconut nectar and the zest and juice of half an orange. Cover the tray with foil. Bake for 10 minutes and then check. The younger and fresher the rhubarb is, the less time it takes to cook so be careful it doesn't become mushy. Mix the rhubarb around and, unless already soft, cover with the foil again and return to the oven for about 5 more minutes or until it is soft and a skewer can easily be inserted into the centre of a piece. Leave to cool.

Place the strawberries in a large bowl. Peel the remaining oranges then cut out the segments with a serrated knife and add to the strawberries. Squeeze in any remaining juice from the orange centres. Add the rest of the vanilla seeds, the orange blossom water and the cooked rhubarb, stirring everything together. Taste and add another tablespoon of honey or coconut nectar if you like.

To make the vanilla cashew 'yogurt', blend all the ingredients until smooth.

Serve the cakes with the compote and 'yogurt' and enjoy. These are best eaten fresh but will keep for up to five days in a sealed container in the fridge, as will the compote and 'yogurt'.

# Cherry and pistachio upside-down cakes with mesquite

*Makes 12 muffin-sized cakes*

60 g (2 oz / scant ½ cup) pistachio
nuts, preferably activated dried
(see page 25)
80 g (2¾ oz / scant ⅔ cup) coconut sugar,
plus 1 tbsp for the bottom of the
moulds
1½ tsp mesquite powder, plus 1 tsp for
the bottom of the moulds
36 sweet cherries, about 360 g
(12¾ oz / 2½ cups)
100 g (3½ oz / 1 cup less 2 tbsp) ground
almonds (almond meal)
50 g (1¾ oz / ⅓ cup) buckwheat flour
1 tsp baking powder
½ tsp Himalyan pink salt
100 g (3½ oz / scant ½ cup) coconut
butter or non-hydrogenated dairy-free
butter, plus extra for greasing
2 eggs

**To serve**
Sweet cherries
Chopped pistachio nuts

*Mesquite is a naturally sweet superfood powder, made from the large bean-like pods of the mesquite tree. It is low-GI, rich in calcium, lysine and magnesium, and has a unique flavour – slightly spicy, sweet and malty with caramel notes. It pairs beautifully with the sweet and juicy cherries submerged in a soft pistachio sponge.*

Preheat the oven to 170°C / 325°F / Gas Mark 3. Grease a 12-hole muffin tin. Line a baking tray with baking parchment.

On the lined baking tray, lightly toast the pistachio nuts for 5–7 minutes until they are just beginning to colour. Leave to cool, then finely chop.

Mix together 1 tbsp coconut sugar with 1 tsp mesquite powder and sprinkle about ¼ tsp of the mix into the bottom of each mould. Stone the cherries, breaking them in half with your fingers as you do so. Fill each muffin mould with three cherries (six halves), arranged in a circle, slightly overlapping. Pour in any extra cherry juices and sprinkle over any leftover sugar and spice mix. Set aside.

Mix together the rest of the sugar and mesquite powder, ground almonds (almond meal), flour, baking powder and salt. Add the chopped pistachio nuts. Melt the butter and add to the dry ingredients, followed by the eggs, and mix well. Divide the mix between the 12 moulds, spooning it on top of the cherries, and bake for 10 minutes, then rotate the tin and bake for a further 2–4 minutes, until the cakes are just firm to touch, slightly golden round the edges and some juices might be bubbling up.

Leave to cool in the tin then remove and top with fresh cherries and chopped pistachio nuts. These cakes are also delightful served with a chunk of homemade chocolate (see page 156), chocolate ice cream or whipped coconut cream (see page 27).

**VARIATIONS**

*Rhubarb and pistachio cakes*
Follow the above recipe, but replace the cherries with 200 g (7 oz) rhubarb, chopped into ½ cm (⅕ inch) pieces, dividing the rhubarb equally between the bottom of the muffin tins. Serve with extra rhubarb compote using the method on page 53 to make the compote.

*Blueberry and pistachio cakes*
Follow the above recipe, but replace the cherries with 180 g (6¼ oz / scant 1¼ cups) of blueberries, divided equally between the muffin tins.

# Hot chocolate chestnut cakes with choco-malt sauce

......................................................................................

*An indulgent and totally nourishing pudding? It does exist, and it's right here! Serve these chocolate gems warm from the oven, pour over the malty chocolate sauce, top with the lightest whipped vanilla cream and your guests will be content, to say the least! They're incredibly easy to make, too.*

......................................................................................

*Makes 8 small cakes*

## Chocolate chestnut cakes

3 tbsp milled flax seeds
9 tbsp hazelnut or almond milk (see page 28)
50 g (1¾ oz / ¼ cup) coconut oil, plus extra for greasing
30 g (1 oz / scant ¼ cup) tinned unsweetened whole peeled chestnuts
55 g (2 oz / generous ⅓ cup) chestnut flour
15 g (½ oz / 3 tbsp) cacao powder
55 g (2 oz / ⅓ cup) Palmyra nectar powder
½ tsp baking powder
½ tsp bicarbonate of soda (baking soda)
½ tsp Himalayan pink salt
1 tsp vanilla extract
20 g (¾ oz) homemade chocolate (see page 156) or dark (bittersweet) chocolate 85–100% cocoa solids, cut into 8 equal chunks, or 8 chocolate coins 85–100% cocoa solids

## Choco-malt sauce

220 ml (7½ fl oz / scant 1 cup) sweet thick cashew milk (see page 28)
2 tbsp cacao powder
3 tsp carob powder
1 tsp maca powder
1 tsp lucuma powder
½ tsp Himalayan pink salt
2 tsp vanilla extract
60 g (2 oz / generous ⅓ cup) dates, soaked in filtered water for 1 hour
50–100 ml (1¾–3½ fl oz / scant ¼ cup–⅓ cup plus 1 tbsp) hazelnut or almond milk (see page 28)
½ tbsp date syrup, optional

## To serve

1 x recipe whipped vanilla coconut cream (see page 27)

Preheat the oven to 170°C / 325°F / Gas Mark 3. Grease 8 muffin moulds with coconut oil.

Soak the milled flax seeds in the hazelnut or almond milk for about 15 minutes to form a gel. Melt the coconut oil. Grate the chestnuts into a large bowl (bits that crumble into small pieces are fine), then add the chestnut flour, cacao powder, Palmyra nectar powder, baking powder, bicarbonate of soda (baking soda) and salt. Mix to combine. Add the melted oil, vanilla extract and flax seed gel and stir to combine everything well to form a thick mix.

Divide the mix between the muffin moulds. You should get about 40 g (1½ oz) of mix per cake. Press in a chocolate chunk or coin, covering it with the mix, and bake for 10 minutes. The tops should feel firm and be slightly cracked and puffed up. A skewer inserted in the centre should come out clean, except for some melted chocolate. Cool for 10 minutes and serve while still warm.

Meanwhile, to make the choco-malt sauce, place the cashew milk in a blender with the cacao, carob, maca, lucuma, salt and vanilla extract and blend on full speed for about 20 seconds. Scrape down the blender and repeat. Drain the dates, add to the blender and blend again until completely smooth. Pour the mix into a saucepan and heat up slowly, adjusting the thickness with hazelnut or almond milk to your preferred consistency. I like it to be thick enough to spoon over the cakes. Taste and sweeten with date syrup if desired.

To serve, run a knife around the edge of each cake, carefully scooping them out onto individual plates. Spoon over a few tablespoons of the warm choco-malt sauce and a spoonful of the whipped vanilla coconut cream and serve immediately. Everything will keep well in the fridge for at least three days. When completely cool these cakes become more like brownies.

### NOTES

*These can be made up to 24 hours in advance, spooned into the moulds and refrigerated until needed. If baking straight from the fridge, allow an extra two minutes in the oven.*

*Any leftover sauce can be made into hot chocolate or 'milk' shakes.*

*I don't add sweeteners to my whipped vanilla coconut cream here, but you can add some blonde coconut nectar or raw clear honey if you wish.*

# Cauliflower chickpea curry cakes with lime and mint raita

*Makes 18 cakes*

### Cauliflower chickpea cakes

1 small red chilli
8 spring onions (scallions)
2 large tomatoes
2 cloves garlic, roughly chopped
20 g (¾ oz/3 tbsp) fresh turmeric, roughly chopped
20 g (¾ oz/3 tbsp) fresh ginger, roughly chopped
½ large cauliflower, florets only
1 tbsp coconut oil or EVCP rapeseed oil
1 tsp ground turmeric
1 tsp yellow mustard seeds
1 tsp fenugreek seeds
300 g (10½ oz/2 cups) cooked chickpeas
150 ml (5 fl oz/scant ⅔ cup) coconut milk, plus more if necessary
Finely grated zest and juice of 1 lime
20 g (¾ oz/scant ½ cup) coriander (cilantro), roughly chopped
75 g (2¾ oz/⅔ cup) gram flour
25 g (¾ oz/scant ¼ cup) milled flax seeds
Salt and black pepper

### Lime and mint raita

250 g (8¾ oz/1 cup) natural coconut yogurt
200 g (7 oz) cucumber
Generous handful finely chopped mint
1 tsp ground cumin
4 tsp lime juice
Pinch cayenne pepper, optional
Himalayan pink salt or coarse sea salt
Black pepper

*These spicy savoury cakes with the fresh-flavoured raita make a very satisfying midweek supper. I like to serve them with a colourful salad made from red cabbage, radish, pomegranate seeds, coriander (cilantro), grated carrot, coconut flakes, pumpkin and sesame seeds. Leftovers can be enjoyed for breakfast with poached eggs.*

Preheat the oven to 200°C/400°F/Gas Mark 6 and line a large baking tray with baking parchment.

Finely chop the chilli and spring onions (scallions) and cube the tomatoes. Using a pestle and mortar, grind the garlic, turmeric and ginger to form a rough paste. Pulse the cauliflower in a food processor until small pieces form resembling breadcrumbs. You need 350 g (12¼ oz) in total.

In a large heavy-bottomed saucepan, heat the oil then add the ground turmeric, mustard and fenugreek seeds. After a few minutes, add the chopped chilli, onion and tomatoes and cook for about 5 minutes or until beginning to colour. Add the garlic paste and continue to cook. When everything has softened and is coloured, add the cauliflower and chickpeas, stirring to coat. Add the coconut milk, lime zest and juice. Heat until the coconut milk just begins to boil and then lower the heat and add the coriander (cilantro), gram flour, milled flax seeds and seasoning. Stir everything to combine on a low heat for a further 5 minutes. If it looks a bit dry, add a little more coconut milk. Remove from the heat, leave to cool slightly and check for seasoning.

To make the raita, put the yogurt into a medium-size bowl. Peel and grate the cucumber, you should get about 160 g (5½ oz) grated weight, and add to the yogurt. Add all the other ingredients, stir and season to taste, adding extra chopped mint and lime if you want.

Make the cauliflower chickpea mix into 18 small cakes in your hands. The mix will feel a little wet but that's normal. Put the cakes onto the lined baking tray and bake for 10 minutes or until golden brown. Remove the tray from the oven, turn each cake over and bake for a further 10 minutes or until golden brown. The outer chickpeas become slightly crunchy while the inside stays perfectly soft. Serve warm with the raita.

The cakes and the raita will keep for five days in a sealed container in the fridge.

# Millet, mushroom and sage risotto cake

*Serves 8–10 with a big salad*

180 g (6¼ oz / scant 1 cup) wholegrain millet

1 tbsp coconut oil or EVCP rapeseed oil

1 garlic clove, crushed or finely chopped

1 red onion, finely chopped

1 litre (35 fl oz / 4¼ cups) vegetable stock, homemade or made with 2 good-quality vegetable stock cubes

500 g (1 lb 2 oz) mixed mushrooms, such as chestnut, buna shimeji, golden enoki and shiitake, chopped

10 sage leaves, finely chopped, plus 15–20 whole sage leaves for topping

Finely grated zest of 1 lemon

Generous grating of nutmeg

1 tsp nutritional yeast flakes

Coarse sea salt

Black pepper

4 eggs

20 g (¾ oz / ⅓ cup) parsley, finely chopped, plus extra for garnishing

*The mild sweetness and nutty flavour of millet goes so well with earthy plump mushrooms and fresh herbs. I like this light but filling protein-rich savoury cake at lunchtime or supper with a big green salad, plus it works well the next morning with sliced avocado, keeping you fuelled until lunch.*

Soak the millet in 500 ml (17 fl oz / 2⅛ cup) of filtered water with 1 tsp of lemon juice or apple cider vinegar for 8–12 hours or overnight, then drain and rinse well.

Preheat the oven to 180°C / 350°F / Gas Mark 4. In a 30 cm (12 inch) oven-proof frying pan (skillet), at least 5 cm (2 inches) deep, melt the oil and then add the garlic and onion, cooking on a medium-high heat for about 3 minutes, until they are starting to brown. Add the millet and stir in – you will notice a nutty flavour developing. Add 250 ml (8½ fl oz / 1 cup) of stock, stir in and simmer for 5 minutes or until the stock has been absorbed. Add half of the mushrooms along with 250 ml (8½ fl oz / 1 cup) more stock. Let the millet soak up all of the liquids and then add another 250 ml (8½ fl oz / 1 cup), again stirring until it has all been soaked up.

Gradually add the rest of the stock, in two batches, and stir in. With the last batch of stock, add the rest of the mushrooms, chopped sage leaves, lemon zest, nutmeg, yeast flakes and seasoning. Cook for about 5 more minutes, stirring and testing it until it is soft but slightly al dente and all the stock has been absorbed. Remove from the heat, taste and add extra seasoning if necessary.

In a large bowl, mix the eggs with the parsley. Gradually add about a quarter of the mushroom millet mix at a time to the eggs, stirring well to combine. When everything has been mixed together, tip it all back into the frying pan (skillet), evening out the top with a palette knife (frosting spatula), top with the whole sage leaves and bake in the oven for about 10–20 minutes until set but with a slight shake.

Serve warm from the oven, sprinkled with extra chopped parsley. Any leftovers will keep well in the fridge for up to three days.

# Muffins, loaf cakes and breads

# Amaranth, berry and banana muffins with buckwheat streusel

........................................................................

*These gorgeously soft muffins are finished off with a crunchy topping of sweetly spiced seeds and buckwheat groats. The amaranth 'porridge' helps to keep the muffins moist, and gives them an interesting texture and an earthy wholesome flavour. Enjoy them warm from the oven for breakfast, brunch or tea.*

........................................................................

*Makes 12 muffins*

## Muffins

75 g (2¾ oz / ⅔ cup) amaranth grain

70 g (2½ oz / scant ½ cup) buckwheat groats

40 g (1½ oz / ¼ cup) pumpkin seeds

40 g (1½ oz / ¼ cup) sunflower seeds

25 g (¾ oz / 2 tbsp) flax seeds

150 ml (5 fl oz / scant ⅔ cup) cold filtered water

75 g (2¾ oz / ½ cup) buckwheat flour

½ tsp ground cinnamon

½ tsp ground mixed spice

1 tsp bicarbonate of soda (baking soda)

½ tsp baking powder

¼ tsp Himalayan pink salt

240 g (8½ oz) banana flesh (about 2 bananas), plus ½ banana for topping

Finely grated zest of 1 orange

2 eggs

70 g (2½ oz / ⅓ cup) coconut nectar

150 ml (5 fl oz / scant ⅔ cup) EVCP rapeseed oil

60 g (2 oz / ½ cup) dried cranberries, cut in half

60 g (2 oz / ½ cup) raspberries, fresh or frozen

60 g (2 oz / generous ⅓ cup) blueberries, fresh or frozen

## Streusel

¼ tsp Himalayan pink salt

½ tsp ground cinnamon

½ tsp mixed spice

1 tbsp coconut nectar

In a glass or ceramic bowl, soak the amaranth for 8–12 hours or overnight in 150 ml (5 fl oz / scant ⅔ cup) of filtered water with ¼ tsp lemon juice or apple cider vinegar. In a separate glass or ceramic bowl, soak the buckwheat groats and all the seeds for 8 hours or overnight in 350 ml (12 fl oz / 1½ cups) of filtered water with ¾ tsp of Himalayan pink salt.

Drain the amaranth using a fine sieve and rinse thoroughly under cold water, then put in a saucepan with the measured water. Bring to the boil and then turn down to a low heat until the seeds have absorbed the water, about 10 minutes, stirring occasionally so they don't catch. When the 'porridge' is cooked, the amaranth should be soft with a very slight 'al dente' bite. Leave to cool.

Meanwhile, drain the groats and seeds using a fine sieve and rinse thoroughly under cold water. Set aside 115 g (4 oz / ¾ cup) of the groat and seed mix for the muffins, and add the rest to the streusel ingredients, mix well and set aside.

Preheat the oven to 170°C / 325°F / Gas Mark 3 and line a muffin tin with 12 cases.

In a small bowl, whisk together the buckwheat flour, cinnamon, mixed spice, bicarbonate of soda (baking soda), baking powder and salt. In a large bowl, mash the banana well with a fork, leaving some small lumps for texture. Add the orange zest, eggs, coconut nectar, oil, all the berries, reserved soaked seeds and groats and cooled amaranth 'porridge' to the banana and mix everything together well. Fold in the dry ingredients until just combined.

Spoon the mix into the cases, making sure each muffin has a fairly even amount of berries. Top each muffin with a ½ cm (⅕ inch) slice of banana, pushing it down vertically into the mix, then sprinkle the streusel equally over the top of the muffins.

Bake for 10 minutes, turn and bake for a further 10 minutes or until the muffins are golden brown and a skewer inserted into the centre comes out clean. Leave to cool for about 10 minutes in their tin then enjoy warm from the oven, with extra granola, fruit and natural yogurt, for breakfast or an afternoon energy-boost.

These keep in the fridge for up to five days and freeze well too.

## Spiced parsnip muffins

*Makes 12 muffins*

200 g (7 oz / 2¼ cups) peeled and grated
  parsnip (about 1 parsnip)
110 g (4 oz / ⅓ cup) maple syrup
100 g (3½ oz / scant ½ cup) easy apple
  purée (see page 32)
150 ml (5 fl oz / scant ⅔ cup) EVCP
  rapeseed oil
3 eggs
Finely grated zest of 1 orange
1 tsp vanilla extract
140 g (5 oz / scant 1 cup) brown rice flour
80 g (2¾ oz / ⅔ cup) millet flour
20 g (¾ oz / 2½ tbsp) arrowroot
1½ tsp baking powder
½ tsp bicarbonate of soda (baking soda)
½ tsp ground cloves
1 tsp ground cinnamon
1 tsp ground ginger
Generous pinch ground
  cardamom
Small grating whole nutmeg
½ tsp Himalayan pink salt
30 g (1 oz / scant ¼ cup) poppy seeds

*When the aroma of these muffins starts to fill your house in the morning, everyone will be jumping out of bed to try one! They're full of nourishing and satisfying ingredients, from the comforting spices to the delightful sweet nutty millet flour.*

Preheat the oven to 170°C / 325°F / Gas Mark 3 and line a muffin tin with 12 cases. In a large bowl, combine everything from the grated parsnip to the vanilla extract. In another large bowl, combine the rest of the dry ingredients from the flours to the poppy seeds and make a well in the centre. Gradually stir in the liquids, slightly folding the mix so you don't knock out too much air.

When well combined, divide the mix between the muffin cases. Bake for about 20 minutes, rotating the tray halfway, until the tops of the muffins are golden brown and just spring back when touched lightly. Leave to cool slightly in the tin and then enjoy while still warm. Keep in an airtight container for at least three days.

### NOTES
*I don't soak the poppy seeds here as they are so small they could fall through some sieves when draining; a small amount of phytic acid is okay (see page 25).*

*If you like more of a subtle spicing, reduce the cinnamon and ginger to ½ tsp of each.*

## Apple and hazelnut muffins

*Makes 8 muffins*

160 ml (5½ fl oz / ⅔ cup) hazelnut milk
  (see page 28)
2 tsp apple cider vinegar
80 g (2¾ oz / scant ⅔ cup) hazelnuts,
  preferably activated dried (see page 25)
80 g (2¾ oz / generous ½ cup) brown rice
  flour
60 g (2 oz / ⅓ cup plus 1 tbsp) teff flour
1 tbsp milled flax seeds
40 g (1½ oz / ⅓ cup) ground hazelnuts
1 tsp baking powder
1 tsp bicarbonate of soda (baking soda)
1 tsp ground cassia or 1–1½ tsp ground
  cinnamon
40 g (1½ oz / ¼ cup) raisins, optional
3–4 dessert apples, such as Cox or
  Ribston Pippin
60 ml (2 fl oz / ¼ cup) EVCP rapeseed oil
60 g (2 oz / ¼ cup) easy apple purée (see
  page 32)
80 g (2¾ oz / ¼ cup) maple syrup

*Cassia is a more robust spice than its sweeter and delicate close relation, cinnamon, and goes wonderfully with malty teff flour, toasted nuts and apple.*

Preheat the oven to 170°C / 325°F / Gas Mark 3. Line a muffin tray with 8 cases and line a baking tray with baking parchment.

Mix together the hazelnut milk and apple cider vinegar. Place the hazelnuts on the lined baking tray and lightly toast for 7 minutes. Leave to cool, remove the skins then chop to medium–small pieces. Combine the flours, flax seeds, ground hazelnuts, baking powder, bicarbonate of soda (baking soda), cassia or cinnamon and raisins. Peel, quarter and core two of the apples. Cut into ½ cm (⅕ inch) cubes – you need 100 g (3½ oz) apple cubes, so cut more if necessary. Add the apple and 60 g (2 oz / ½ cup) of the chopped hazelnuts to the dry ingredients and make a well in the centre.

Combine the rapeseed oil, apple purée and maple syrup with the hazelnut milk mix, add to the dry ingredients, and lightly fold until well combined. Divide the mix between the 8 cases. Cut the rest of the apples into quarters (do not peel), core them and then cut 16 ½–1 cm (⅕–⅓ inch) slices, pressing in 2 slices to the top of each muffin. Sprinkle the remaining chopped hazelnuts over the muffins. Bake for about 20 minutes, rotating the tin halfway through the cooking time, until the muffins are golden brown and a skewer inserted into the centre of a muffin comes out clean. Leave to cool for a few minutes, and then enjoy while still warm. These muffins will last well for three days in an airtight container.

# Coconut and carrot muffins with cacao-maca-lucuma 'yogurt'

·······································································

*These coconut-packed muffins are dense with goodness, as muffins should be, but soft at the same time. I am always surprised at how much moisture coconut flour absorbs – as you'll see, a little goes a long way. Grab one for breakfast if you're in a rush or enjoy them for brunch or pudding with this extra creamy chocolate 'yogurt'.*

·······································································

*Makes 12 muffins*

60 g (2 oz / generous ¼ cup) coconut oil

6 eggs

4 tbsp coconut milk

100 g (3½ oz / scant ½ cup) coconut
  nectar

2 tsp vanilla extract

1 tsp Himalayan pink salt

70 g (2½ oz / ⅔ cup) coconut flour

½ tsp baking powder

100 g (3½ oz / generous 1 cup) grated
  carrot

30 g (1 oz / ⅓ cup) desiccated coconut,
  plus extra for topping

**Cacao-maca-lucuma 'yogurt'**

1 x recipe cashew cream (see page 27)

6 tsp cacao powder

1½ tsp lucuma powder

1½ tsp maca powder

20 g (¾ oz / scant 1 tbsp) date syrup, or
  other sweetener

¼ vanilla pod (bean), split lengthways
  and seeds scraped out

2 tsp lemon juice

Pinch Himalayan pink salt

30 g (1 oz) homemade chocolate (see
  page 156) or dark (bittersweet)
  chocolate 85% cocoa solids

Preheat the oven to 170°C / 325°F / Gas Mark 3 and line a muffin tray with 12 cases.

Melt the coconut oil. Whisk the oil with the eggs, coconut milk, coconut nectar, vanilla extract and salt. Sieve in the coconut flour and baking powder and whisk until smooth and most of the lumps are gone. Add the grated carrot and desiccated coconut and stir once more.

Spoon into the cases, sprinkle with dessicated coconut and bake for 20 minutes, rotating halfway, until the tops are golden brown, firm to touch and bounce back when you press them lightly. Leave to cool in the tin.

To make the cacao-maca-lucuma 'yogurt', blend everything together except for the chocolate until smooth. Taste and adjust the sweetness if necessary. Chop up the chocolate to make chocolate chips and mix into the 'yogurt'.

Serve the 'yogurt' with the coconut muffins and store any leftover in a sealed glass jar in the fridge, where it will keep for at least four days, as will the muffins.

# Polenta (cornmeal) muffins with spinach, sun-dried tomatoes and olives

**Makes 12 muffins**

30 ml (1 fl oz/2 tbsp) apple cider vinegar

150 ml (5 fl oz/scant ⅔ cup) almond milk (see page 28)

180 g (6¼ oz/generous 1 cup) quick-cook polenta (cornmeal)

120 g (4¼ oz/generous ¾ cup) brown rice flour

30 g (1 oz/¼ cup) arrowroot

1 tsp coarse sea salt, finely ground

1½ tsp baking powder

1½ tsp bicarbonate of soda (baking soda)

¼ tsp dried chilli flakes, optional

60 g (2 oz/½ cup) gram flour

60 ml (2 fl oz/¼ cup) filtered water

36 large basil leaves (about 30 g/1 oz/ generous 1 cup), finely chopped

1½ garlic cloves, finely chopped

75 g (2¾ oz/1⅓ cups) sun-dried tomatoes, chopped into pea-size pieces, plus 30 g (1 oz/scant ½ cup) for topping

75 g (2¾ oz/½ cup) black olives, quartered

60 g (2 oz/scant ½ cup) pine nuts

120 ml (4 fl oz/½ cup) EVCP rapeseed oil

60 g (2 oz/2 cups) baby-leaf spinach leaves, roughly shredded into quarters

*Baking these moreish muffins makes me think of summer. Serve them warm from the oven with a salad for a light al fresco lunch or picnic. With the polenta (cornmeal) and pine nuts they are deliciously crumbly and crunchy at the same time, and are packed with flavour from the rich tomatoes, salty olives and basil, with a chilli kick at the end.*

Preheat the oven to 170°C/325°F/Gas Mark 3. Line a muffin tin with 12 pieces of baking parchment, each about 15 cm (6 inch) square, which make attractive cases, or 12 standard muffin cases.

In a measuring jug, mix the vinegar with the almond milk and set aside (after a few minutes it will resemble thin buttermilk).

In a large bowl, combine the polenta (cornmeal), rice flour, arrowroot, salt, baking powder, bicarbonate of soda (baking soda) and chilli flakes, if using, and make a well in the centre. In another bowl, mix the gram flour with the water to make a paste.

Mix the basil, garlic, chopped sun-dried tomatoes, olives and half the pine nuts with the rapeseed oil. Pour the oil mix, milk and vinegar mix and the gram paste into the dry ingredients. Sprinkle the spinach over the top and then stir everything lightly together to combine. The mix will be quite wet and should stick together well.

Spoon the mix into the muffin cases, dividing it between the 12 cases. Top each muffin with a whole piece of sun-dried tomato, pressing it down slightly into the muffin mix otherwise it will burn. Sprinkle the remaining pine nuts over the muffins, pushing them in slightly, too.

Bake for 10 minutes, rotate the tray and cook for a further 5 minutes, or until a skewer inserted into the centre of a muffin comes out clean. The tops should be golden; the nuts lightly toasted.

Cool for 5 minutes in the tin. Serve immediately when still warm or remove from the tin and leave to cool on a wire rack. These are best eaten fresh but will keep in an airtight container for at least three days. They are also good warmed in the oven for about 5 minutes at a low temperature.

# Purple haze loaf with super-berry cashew 'yogurt'

........................................................................................

*Fabulous flavour, health-boosting ingredients and lots of colour – enjoy this soft and milky loaf for breakfast or brunch served with the luxuriously creamy antioxidant-rich super-berry 'yogurt' and fresh fruit. It also works well toasted and drizzled with maple syrup or spread with coconut oil, nut butter or chia jam (jelly) (see page 32).*

........................................................................................

*Serves 8–10*

**Purple haze loaf**
2 tbsp milled flax seeds
6 tbsp filtered water
150 g (5¼ oz / 1 cup) buckwheat flour
1 tsp baking powder
1 tsp bicarbonate of soda (baking soda)
½ tsp Himalayan pink salt
100 g (3½ oz / ⅓ cup) maple syrup
70 ml (2½ fl oz / ¼ cup plus 2 tsp)
  almond milk (see page 28)
½ vanilla pod (bean), split lengthways
  and seeds scraped out
75 g (2¾ oz / ⅓ cup) coconut oil, melted,
  plus extra for greasing
25 g (¾ oz / ¼ cup) purple corn flour
80 g (2¾ oz / generous ¾ cup)
  blackcurrants, fresh or frozen
80 g (2¾ oz / ½ cup) blueberries, fresh
  or frozen
80 g (2¾ oz / ½ cup) dried blueberries,
  unsweetened

**Super-berry cashew 'yogurt'**
1 x recipe cashew cream (see page 27)
40 ml (1½ fl oz / 8 tsp) lemon juice
2 tsp acai berry powder
2 tsp purple corn flour
½ vanilla pod (bean), split lengthways
  and seeds scraped out, or 1 tsp vanilla
  extract
150 g (5¼ oz / 1 cup) fresh blueberries
Up to 30 g (1 oz / 1½ tbsp) raw honey or
  coconut nectar, optional
40 goji berries (heaped 1 tbsp)

Preheat the oven to 170°C / 325°F / Gas Mark 3. Grease a 24 x 8 x 8 cm deep (9¾ x 3 x 3 inch) loaf tin with coconut oil and line the bottom of the tin with baking parchment.

Mix the milled flax seeds with the water and leave for 15 minutes to form a gel. Stir now and again. Combine the buckwheat flour, baking powder, bicarbonate of soda (baking soda) and salt. Whisk lightly to remove any lumps. Combine the maple syrup, almond milk and vanilla seeds. Make a well in the centre of the dry ingredients and pour in the milk mix, followed by the coconut oil. Mix lightly to combine and then fold in the flax seed mix.

Add the purple corn flour, blackcurrants and all the blueberries and fold again until just combined. Pour the mix into the prepared tin and spread out. Bake for 20 minutes, rotate the tin and reduce the heat to 130°C / 250°F / Gas Mark ½, baking for a further 20–30 minutes or until the top has formed a golden-brown crust and a skewer inserted into the centre of the loaf comes out clean. Leave to cool on a wire rack in the tin for about 30 minutes, then remove from the tin.

For the 'yogurt', place the cashew cream in a blender and add the lemon juice, acai berry powder, purple corn flour and vanilla and blend. Add the fresh blueberries and blend once more until everything is well combined and totally smooth, scraping down and repeating if necessary. The mix should now be a lovely purple colour. Try the 'yogurt' and add your preferred liquid sweetener to taste, if you like, and more lemon if necessary. Pour the 'yogurt' into a bowl and then gently stir in the goji berries (but do not blend). Serve alongside the loaf.

The loaf is lovely eaten fresh on the day it is baked, preferably warm from the oven. It will keep in an airtight container in the fridge for at least four days, as will the 'yogurt'.

### NOTES
*Purple corn flour is a South American cooking staple made from a purple variety of corn and is extremely high in anthocyanins. It adds a dark hue to baked goods and can be used raw too, adding a pretty purple colour to food, as in this 'yogurt' recipe.*

*Acai berry powder is made from the berries of the acai – a palm tree. It retains an optimal number of its naturally occurring nutrients, including fibre, vitamin A, calcium, iron, amino acids and omega 6 and omega 9 fatty acids and it is particularly high in antioxidants. It is great added to smoothies too.*

# Baked banana, date and pecan loaf with spiced caramel sauce

*Served at breakfast with yogurt, with a cup of tea in the afternoon, or for pudding with custard, this is the ideal anytime cake. The mix of the dates, caramel-sweet banana, treacly teff flour and molasses make this sticky toffee pudding-like cake rich, moist and devilishly good, its flavours enlivened by the spices in the divine sauce.*

*Serves 8–10*

**Banana loaf**

1 tbsp milled flax seeds
3 tbsp filtered water
80 ml (2¾ fl oz / ⅓ cup) cashew milk
  (see page 28)
1 tsp apple cider vinegar
190 g (6¾ oz / 1¼ cups) dates
190 ml (6¾ fl oz / ¾ cup) filtered water
2 tsp bicarbonate of soda (baking soda)
2–3 large bananas
120 g (4¼ oz / generous 1 cup) pecans,
  preferably activated dried (see
  page 25)
70 g (2½ oz / ½ cup) teff flour
70 g (2½ oz / ½ cup) brown rice flour
20 g (¾ oz / 2½ tbsp) arrowroot
¼ tsp baking powder
¼ tsp ground cinnamon
½ tsp ground cardamom
½ tsp mixed spice
½ tsp coarse sea salt, ground
50 g (1¾ oz / scant ¼ cup) easy apple
  purée (see page 32)
40 g (1½ oz / 2 tbsp) unsulphured
  molasses
80 ml (2¾ fl oz / ⅓ cup) EVCP rapeseed
  oil
1 tsp vanilla extract

**Spiced caramel sauce**

1 x 400 ml (14 fl oz) can coconut milk
100 g (3½ oz / ⅓ cup) maple syrup or
  raw honey
½ tsp coarse sea salt
½ vanilla pod (bean), split lengthways
  and seeds scraped out, pod (bean)
  kept
5 g (scant ¼ oz / about 4) whole star
  anise
5 g (scant ¼ oz / 1 tbsp) cardamom pods

Preheat the oven to 200°C / 400°F / Gas Mark 6. Grease and line the bottom of an 18 x 11 x 8 cm deep (7 x 4¼ x 3 inch) loaf tin with baking parchment. Combine the milled flax seeds with the water and leave for about 15 minutes to form a gel. Mix the cashew milk with the apple cider vinegar and set aside.

In a medium saucepan, cook the dates with the measured water until all the water is soaked up and forms a paste. This should take no longer than 5 minutes. When the water has just been soaked up, remove the pan immediately from the heat and stir in 1 tsp bicarbonate of soda (baking soda). The mixture will fizz. Keep on mixing until most of the fizzing has stopped then leave the paste to cool.

On a baking tray, bake the bananas in the oven for about 3 minutes on each side until the skins blacken. Remove from the oven and turn down the temperature to 170°C / 325°F / Gas Mark 3, then toast the pecans on a baking tray for 5–7 minutes, until just beginning to colour. When cooled, roughly chop.

In a large bowl, combine all the dry ingredients from the teff flour to the salt and add the remaining 1 tsp bicarbonate of soda (baking soda). Peel the bananas and mash 200 g (7 oz / scant 1 cup) into the dates. Add the apple purée, molasses, oil and vanilla extract to the cashew milk. Make a well in the centre of the dry ingredients and add the cashew milk mix, dates and bananas, flax seed gel and chopped pecans. Mix thoroughly to combine by lightly folding everything together. Pour into the prepared tin and bake for 30 minutes, rotating the tin halfway. Reduce the heat to 160°C / 310°F / Gas Mark 2½ and bake for a further 15–20 minutes, or until a skewer inserted in the centre of the loaf comes out clean. Leave the loaf to cool in the tin while you make the sauce, then demould when cooled completely.

In a medium saucepan bring all the sauce ingredients to a boil, stirring to combine. Turn down the heat to a medium rolling boil and reduce the sauce for 10 minutes, stirring now and again so it doesn't catch. It will be looking thicker and have become a golden caramel colour. Remove the cardamom pods, star anise and vanilla pod (bean) with a slotted spoon. Pour into a bowl and set aside.

When ready to serve, give the sauce a good whisk, pour it into a jug and serve generously over slices of the loaf with extra chopped pecans if you wish. You can serve the loaf and the sauce either warmed up or cold. The loaf will keep in a sealed container for up to five days.

**NOTE**
*Molasses is made from sugar cane, containing all the vitamins, minerals and fibre that white sugar is stripped of. A real energy booster that is especially rich in zinc, it is a dark treacle which is full of flavour and adds deep colour and richness to cakes and breads. Only small amounts are needed, as it is quite strong. Buy pure cane molasses.*

# Extra fruity fruit loaf

....................................................................................................

*Serves 10–12*

## Fruit loaf

60 g (2 oz / ⅓ cup plus 1 tbsp) currants

60 g (2 oz / generous ⅓ cup) sultanas
  (seedless golden raisins)

60 g (2 oz / ⅓ cup) raisins

90 g (3 oz / scant ⅔ cup) dried figs, stalks
  removed

90 g (3 oz / scant ⅔ cup) unsulphured
  dried apricots

90 g (3 oz / scant ⅔ cup) dates

Zest and 60 ml (2 fl oz / ¼ cup) juice of
  1 lemon

Zest and 60 ml (2 fl oz / ¼ cup) juice of
  1 orange

1 vanilla pod (bean), cut in half
  lengthways, seeds scraped out, pod
  (bean) kept

60 g (2 oz / 3 tbsp) maple syrup

300 ml (10½ fl oz / 1¼ cups) tea, made
  using 1 loose-leaf Darjeeling tea
  pyramid and 1 chai tea pyramid (see
  note)

125 g (4½ oz / ¾ cup plus scant 2 tbsp)
  whole almonds

135 g (4¾ oz / 1 cup less 2 tbsp)
  buckwheat flour

135 g (4¾ oz / 1 cup) chestnut flour

5 tsp arrowroot

20 g (¾ oz / 3 tbsp) gram flour

60 g (2 oz / ½ cup) coconut sugar

1½ tsp mixed spice

1½ tsp baking powder

1 tsp bicarbonate of soda (baking soda)

¼ tsp Himalayan pink salt

75 g (2¾ oz / ⅓ cup) coconut oil

## Glaze

3 plums, destoned (100 g / 3½ oz
  without stones), fresh or frozen

5 tbsp unsweetened apple juice

20 g (¾ oz / 1 tbsp) raw honey or
  coconut nectar

Or about 30 g (1 oz / 2 tbsp) no added
  sugar high fruit content apricot jam
  (jelly)

*When it's cold, there's nothing quite like a slice of gorgeous dark fruit loaf with a big mug of tea. This cakey moist loaf is light but still rich, wholesome and bursting with sweet fruits and crunchy almonds. Bake it in a round 18–20 cm (7–8 inch) loose-bottomed cake tin for a great 'free-from' Christmas cake, and it's vegan, too.*

....................................................................................................

Place the currants, sultanas (seedless golden raisins), raisins, figs, apricots and dates in a large glass or ceramic bowl with the citrus zests and juice, vanilla seeds and pod (bean), maple syrup and tea. Submerge the tea pyramids in the fruit for maximum flavour. Leave to soak overnight, but not for more than 12 hours otherwise there will be no liquid left to bind the cake mix. In a separate glass or ceramic bowl, soak the almonds in 250 ml (8½ fl oz / 1 cup) of filtered water with ½ tsp of Himalayan pink salt for 8–12 hours (or overnight).

Preheat the oven to 170°C / 325°F / Gas Mark 3. Line the bottom and sides of an 18 x 11 x 8 cm deep (7 x 4¼ x 3 inch) loaf tin with baking parchment. In a large bowl, combine all the dry ingredients from the buckwheat flour to the salt.

Drain, rinse thoroughly and set aside 50 g (1¾ oz / ⅓ cup) of the almonds for the top. In a food processor, roughly process the rest of the almonds, keeping some larger pieces for texture. Add to the dry ingredients.

Place the soaked figs, apricots and dates in a food processor and process until half pulp, half still whole. Add to the dry ingredients. Remove the vanilla pod (bean) and tea pyramids from the soaking liquids, squeezing them out over the bowl for extra flavour, then discard. Add the rest of the soaked fruit and liquid to the dry ingredients and processed fruit. Finally melt the coconut oil and stir it in, mixing until everything is well combined. Pour into the tin and spread into the corners with a knife. Bang the tin lightly a few times on your work surface. Place the reserved almonds around the edge of the cake, gently pressing them into the mix.

Bake for 20 minutes. Turn down the heat to 160°C / 310°F / Gas Mark 2½, rotate and bake for a further 40 minutes, turning again halfway, until the top is golden-brown and slightly bounces back if touched; a skewer inserted in the centre should come out clean. Leave to cool completely in the tin.

To make the glaze, bring the plums, apple juice and honey or coconut nectar to the boil and boil for about 5 minutes, breaking up the plums with a spoon. Turn down to a simmer for 5 more minutes until thick and glossy. Remove from the heat. Turn out the cake when completely cool and use a pastry brush to brush the glaze (or apricot jam (jelly), if using) over the cake.

Stored in a sealed container, this will keep well for at least five days. I store it in the fridge as it keeps better and becomes even softer. It also freezes well.

### NOTE

*For a warming, spicy, festive flavour, use 1 bag of black tea, such as Darjeeling, brewed with 1 bag of chai tea, which contains a delicious mix of black tea, cardamom, cinnamon and ginger. Teapigs make a great chai tea blend with no additives or sweeteners. You can use regular tea bags, but I use pyramid bags as they contain loose leaves, so have great flavour, and are less likely to rip or break than regular tea bags.*

# Apricot, cranberry and almond tea bread

*This tea bread always goes down really well. It's not too sweet and it's slightly drier than a cake, as a tea bread should be, but the cranberries and apricots balance everything out with their moist chewiness and robust sharp and sweet flavours. The combination of the brown rice and sorghum flours make it wholesomely light, while the yogurt adds a soft creaminess.*

*Serves 10–12*

60 g (2 oz / scant ½ cup) almonds, preferably activated dried (see page 25)

100 g (3½ oz / scant ⅔ cup) unsulphured dried apricots

70 g (2½ oz / generous ½ cup) dried cranberries

100 g (3½ oz / 1 cup less 2 tbsp) ground almonds (almond meal)

105 g (3¾ oz / ⅔ cup) brown rice flour

40 g (1½ oz / ⅓ cup) sorghum flour

15 g (½ oz / 2 tbsp) cornflour (cornstarch)

15 g (½ oz / 2 tbsp) arrowroot

70 g (2½ oz / scant ½ cup) Palmyra nectar powder

½ tsp Himalayan pink salt

½ tsp baking powder

½ tsp bicarbonate of soda (baking soda)

½ tsp ground cloves

2 eggs

190 g (6¾ oz / ¾ cup) natural coconut yogurt

Zest of ½ lemon

Zest of 1 orange

50 g (1¾ oz / ¼ cup) coconut oil

Preheat the oven to 170°C / 325°F / Gas Mark 3 and line a baking tray with baking parchment. Grease and line the bottom of an 18 x 11 x 8 cm deep (7 x 4¼ x 3 inch) loaf tin with baking parchment.

Spread out the almonds on the lined baking tray and toast for 7 minutes, or until they are just taking colour, leave to cool then roughly chop. Chop the apricots into rough pea-sized pieces and mix with the toasted almonds and cranberries.

Combine all the dry ingredients from the ground almonds (almond meal) to the ground cloves. Whisk to disperse any lumps then add in the dried fruit and nut mix.

Mix together the eggs, yogurt and citrus zest. Melt the coconut oil and mix in. Make a well in the centre of the dry ingredients and add in the liquids, mixing to combine.

Tip the mix into the prepared tin, spread the top with a palette knife (frosting spatula) until smooth and even, and bake for about 50 minutes, turning halfway, until the top is golden brown and a skewer inserted in the centre of the loaf comes out clean. If the top is looking too brown, lower the oven temperature to 160°C / 310°F / Gas Mark 2½ during the last 10 minutes of baking. Leave to cool in the tin for 20 minutes, then serve warm with tea. I love to spread slices with coconut oil or almond butter.

This loaf freezes well and will keep for up to five days in an airtight container in the fridge. When it is less fresh, it is lovely warmed up slightly in the oven.

### VARIATION

*Almond tea bread*

If you want a lower-sugar loaf, remove the dried fruits for a deliciously milky flavoured almond tea bread, increasing the amount of almonds if you like.

# Fig and ginger tea bread with dark (bittersweet) chocolate spread

......................................................................................................

*Honeyed dried figs and dark (bittersweet) chocolate chunks, who could resist them together, immersed in a heady tea bread with a soft fiery warmth from fresh ginger? Not overly sweet, serve this tea bread for breakfast or tea, spread thickly with the dark (bittersweet) chocolate spread, or warm up a slice and enjoy with nut butters.*

......................................................................................................

*Serves 10–12*

**Tea bread**

2 tsp loose-leaf strong-flavoured black tea such as Darjeeling, Assam or Earl Grey

200 ml (7 fl oz / generous ¾ cup) boiling water

200 g (7 oz / 1¼ cups) dried figs, small stalks removed

Zest of 1 orange

1 tsp ground cardamom

70 g (2½ oz / ½ cup) Palmyra nectar powder

20 g (¾ oz / 3 tbsp) fresh ginger, finely chopped

100 g (3½ oz / ¾ cup) chestnut flour

100 g (3½ oz / ⅔ cup) buckwheat flour

15 g (½ oz / 2 tbsp) gram flour

10 g (⅓ oz / 1¼ tbsp) arrowroot

½ tsp baking powder

½ tsp Himalayan pink salt

90 g (3 oz) homemade chocolate (see page 156) or dark (bittersweet) chocolate 85% cocoa solids, roughly chopped into small chunks

1 egg or 60 g (2 oz / ¼ cup) easy apple purée (see page 32)

**Dark (bittersweet) chocolate spread**

100 ml (3½ fl oz / ⅓ cup plus 1 tbsp) water

60 g (2 oz / ⅓ cup plus 1 tbsp) Palmyra nectar powder

100 g (3½ oz) homemade chocolate (see page 156 and note below) or dark (bittersweet) chocolate 85% cocoa solids

Brew the tea in the measured boiling water for 4–6 minutes, then strain. Make sure you still have 200 ml (7 fl oz / generous ¾ cup) of tea by really squeezing the leaves or add a little extra water if necessary. In a large bowl, mix together the figs, orange zest, ground cardamom, Palymra nectar powder and ginger. Pour the tea over the fruit and let the mix soak for 8 hours or overnight.

Preheat the oven to 170°C / 325°F / Gas Mark 3 and line the bottom and sides of a 19 x 9 x 6 cm deep (7½ x 3½ x 2½ inch) loaf tin with baking parchment.

Mix together all the dry ingredients and the chocolate pieces. Chop up the figs into small–medium pieces – I do this with scissors while in their soaking liquid. Add the soaked figs, spices and soaking liquids to the dry ingredients. Add the egg or apple purée and mix together thoroughly. Pour into the prepared tin and bake for 20 minutes.

Turn down the heat to 160°C / 310°F / Gas Mark 2½, turn and bake for a further 30 minutes, turning again halfway, until the top is golden-brown and slightly cracking; a skewer inserted in the centre should come out clean except with a little melted chocolate. Leave to cool in the tin completely.

To make the dark (bittersweet) chocolate spread, in a saucepan bring the water and Palmyra nectar powder to a strong rolling boiling, making sure the powder is dissolved. Melt the chocolate in a bain-marie (see page 156). Gradually pour the sweet hot water over the chocolate, incorporating as you do so. When a smooth emulsion has formed, cover the mix to the surface with baking parchment and refrigerate for 1 hour to set softly. The ganache should have a slight shake to it, otherwise it will be too solid to spread. Remove from the fridge and keep in a cool place.

Serve the chocolate spread in a bowl or pot alongside the tea bread and spread generously over slices. The loaf will keep for at least five days in a sealed container (it actually gets better with age), as will the spread. Slices warmed or slightly toasted are great.

### NOTES

*Do not agitate the chocolate mix with a spoon or whisk once made or it will split. If you are worried it looks split, don't panic as it will still taste smooth.*

*The great thing about this loaf is that if you have run out of eggs or apple purée, it will still work. The mix will be a little firmer if you omit these ingredients, so press it well into the tin.*

*The dark (bittersweet) chocolate spread will take longer to set, at least overnight in the fridge, if made with homemade chocolate.*

# Go-to wholegrain gluten-free bread

**Serves 8**

25 g (¾ oz / 2½ tbsp) buckwheat or brown rice flakes

150 ml (5 fl oz / scant ⅔ cup) almond milk (see page 28)

1 tsp apple cider vinegar

90 g (3 oz / ⅔ cup) teff flour

75 g (2¾ oz / ½ cup) brown rice flour

75 g (2¾ oz / ½ cup) buckwheat flour

1 tsp coarse sea salt, finely ground between your fingers

½ tsp bicarbonate of soda (baking soda)

½ tsp baking powder

40 g (1½ oz / generous ¼ cup) sunflower seeds, preferably soaked for 8 hours or activated dried (see page 25)

1½ tsp EVCP rapeseed oil, plus extra for greasing

15 g (½ oz / 2 tsp) unsulphured molasses

½ tsp xanthan gum

2 eggs

*With its rich dark flavours from the wholegrain flours and the treacly, malty molasses, this loaf reminds me of Irish soda bread, one of my favourite types of bread. It has a wonderful cracked crust on the outside, while the middle is slightly soft, and every mouthful feels totally nutritious, wholesome and very delicious indeed.*

Preheat the oven to 170°C / 325°F / Gas Mark 3. Grease a 17 x 10 x 6.5 cm deep (6¾ x 4 x 2½ inch) loaf tin with a little rapeseed oil, line the bottom with baking parchment and then cover the bottom and sides with the buckwheat or brown rice flakes, swirling around in the tin to coat well. A lot of the flakes will not stick, so pour these out and reserve for the top of the loaf.

Mix the almond milk with the apple cider vinegar to make a buttermilk-like liquid. Set aside. Combine the flours with the sea salt, bicarbonate of soda (baking soda) and baking powder and whisk lightly to evenly combine the ingredients and disperse any lumps. Add the sunflower seeds.

Add the oil, molasses and xanthan to the milk and mix with a hand-held blender. Do not over-blend, you just need to pulse the blender a few times to mix the liquids and dissolve the gum. Whisk in the eggs then add this mixture to the dry ingredients, stirring until everything is well combined.

Pour into the tin, smooth the top with the back of a spoon and gently shake the loaf to get rid of any air bubbles. Top with the remaining flakes, pressing them into the dough slightly. Bake for 20 minutes then turn down the oven to 150°C / 300°F / Gas Mark 2 and bake for a further 10 minutes. Using an oven glove, turn out the loaf, putting it upside down onto a baking tray, and bake for a final 10 minutes. A skewer inserted in the centre should come out clean, and when tapped on the bottom the loaf should sound hollow and feel light.

Enjoy this loaf when fresh, or it will keep for up to five days and freezes well too. It toasts superbly and I recommend toasting it to bring out its full flavour.

**NOTES**

*You can make this with other seeds or nuts, or leave the seeds out entirely.*

*This loaf is incredibly versatile and goes well with everything – at breakfast with butter and jam (jelly) or scrambled eggs and grilled (broiled) tomatoes; at lunch with a salad or as a smorgasbord with cured fish and gherkins; in the evening with soup or a stew; or for sandwiches.*

# Sweet potato cornbread

*Make this moreish cornbread for a barbecue – serve with lots of salads, fresh grilled (broiled) fish, local meat and corn on the cob, and all your friends will be happy. Under a perfect crunchy golden crust, the potato adds lightness and a soft sweet depth of flavour, while the spring onions (scallions) and hint of chilli keep it most definitely savoury.*

**Serves 10–12**

About 500 g (1 lb 2 oz) sweet potatoes, with skin on

110 ml (3¾ fl oz / scant ½ cup) almond milk (see page 28)

1 tsp apple cider vinegar

210 g (7½ oz / 1¼ cups) fine / quick-cook polenta (cornmeal)

190 g (6¾ oz / 1¼ cups) brown rice flour

20 g (¾ oz / 2½ tbsp) arrowroot

½ tsp guar gum

1½ tsp baking powder

1½ tsp bicarbonate of soda (baking soda)

2 tsp coarse sea salt, finely ground

30 g (1 oz) thinly sliced spring onions (scallions), about 3–4 small spring onions (scallions)

½ small red chilli, finely sliced

90 ml (3 fl oz / generous ⅓ cup) EVCP rapeseed oil, plus extra for greasing

2 eggs

Preheat the oven to 200°C / 400°F / Gas Mark 6.

Scrub the potatoes and bake for about 30 minutes until the skin(s) have shrivelled and they feel slightly soft. Cut in half and spoon out the flesh to get 300 g (10½ oz / 1½ cups) cooked sweet potato (no skin). Set aside to cool.

Turn the oven down to 190°C / 375°F / Gas Mark 5 and line the bottom of a loose-bottomed 20 cm (8 inch) round cake tin with baking parchment. Grease the edges of the tin with rapeseed oil.

Combine the almond milk and apple cider vinegar. In a large bowl, combine all the dry ingredients from the polenta (cornmeal) to the sea salt and whisk to disperse any lumps. Add the spring onions (scallions) and chilli and mix in.

Mash the sweet potato in a bowl with a fork and add the rapeseed oil and eggs, whisking to combine. Pour in the almond milk mixture and stir once more. Make a well in the centre of the dry ingredients and gradually pour in the potato and milk mix, folding everything together until combined.

Pour the mix into the prepared tin, smooth the top with a small palette knife (frosting spatula) and bake for 20 minutes, rotating the bread halfway. Reduce the heat to 180°C / 350°F / Gas Mark 4 and bake for a further 10 minutes. It is cooked when the top is starting to take on a golden colour, the loaf is firm to the touch and a skewer inserted in the centre comes out clean. Cool for about 10 minutes in the tin on a wire rack then carefully remove from the tin and slice. Serve generous slices warm from the oven with lashings of coconut oil or organic butter.

Keeps for up to five days in an airtight container.

# Waste not, want not multi-seed quinoa bread

*One of the best and yummiest ways to use up all your leftover juice and nut milk pulp is in this bread. The pulp still has a lot of flavour and nutrients, not to mention its healthy fibre. In this vegan loaf, the vegetable pulp adds both freshness and blasts of colour, while the seeds and quinoa flour provide a distinct nutty, earthy flavour.*

**Juice serves 1–2**
**Bread serves 12+**

**Fennel, carrot and ginger juice**
*Makes about 250–300 g (8¾–10½ oz/ compact 1¾ cups) juice pulp*
1 large carrot (185 g / 6½ oz)
2 celery stalks (125 g / 4½ oz)
1 fennel bulb (240 g / 8½ oz)
1 apple (125 g / 4½ oz)
20 g (¾ oz / 3 tbsp) ginger
Juice of 1 lemon

**Quinoa bread**
2 tbsp chia seeds
6 tbsp filtered water
250–300 g (8¾–10½ oz / compact 1¾ cups) juice pulp (see recipe above)
200 g (7 oz / compact 1⅛ cups) almond or hazelnut milk pulp from 1 x recipe nut milk (see page 28)
100 g (3½ oz / ¾ cup plus 1 tbsp) quinoa flour
1 tsp Himalayan pink salt
1 tsp bicarbonate of soda (baking soda)
1 tsp baking powder
2 tbsp psyllium husk powder
80 g (2¾ oz / ½ cup) pumpkin seeds, preferably soaked for 8 hours or activated dried (see page 25)
80 g (2¾ oz / ½ cup plus 1 tbsp) sunflower seeds, preferably soaked for 8 hours or activated dried (see page 25)

### Fennel, carrot and ginger juice
Juice all the ingredients, except the lemon, then stir in the lemon juice at the end. Enjoy the juice and use the pulp in the bread. Everybody's juicers vary, but if you, like me, get large pieces of vegetable chunks in the pulp, do not worry as they add a flavoursome and colourful surprise when eating the bread.

### Quinoa bread
Preheat the oven to 160°C / 310°F / Gas Mark 2½ and grease and line the bottom of a 21 x 11 x 6 cm deep (8¼ x 4¼ x 2½ inch) loaf tin with baking parchment.

Combine the chia seeds and measured water and leave for 15 minutes to form a gel. Put both pulps into a large bowl and add all of the other ingredients along with the chia gel and drained soaked seeds. Mix the dough with your hands, squeezing it through your fingers. With the moisture from the pulps, it should be just wet enough to stick together. Put the dough into the prepared tin, pressing it down well into the corners. Dip your fingers in water then smooth out the top of the loaf with your fingertips.

Bake for about 40 minutes, rotating the loaf after the first 20 minutes. Then, using an oven glove, remove the loaf from the tin, carefully run a knife around the edges, turn it upside down onto a baking tray and remove the baking parchment from the bottom of the loaf. Bake it upside down on the baking tray for another 10 minutes. When it is ready a skewer inserted in the centre should come out clean, the bottom should sound hollow when tapped, and the top should be a golden brown. Leave to cool completely.

Due to its moisture from the wet pulps, this bread is quite moist so it is best eaten thinly sliced and toasted. It can be kept in the fridge for at least four days and freezes well. Freeze in slices and toast straight from the freezer.

*NOTES*
*If you do not have the exact quantities of either the juice or nut pulp, just increase one or the other to add up to 450–500 g (1 lb–1 lb 2 oz) in total, or you can add extra ground almonds (almond meal), which have been moistened with some water, again to add up to 450–500 g (1 lb–1 lb 2 oz). If you only have the nut milk pulp, halve the rest of the ingredients, except for the flour, and follow the recipe above but bake for 10 minutes less than stated above.*

*This loaf also works with buckwheat flour in place of the quinoa. Then try adding a handful or two of activated buckwheat groats. If the mix looks too dry add a little water.*

*For a nutty, grain-free version, replace the quinoa flour with chestnut flour or ground almonds (almond meal), or a combination of both flours, and add a nut mix such as dried activated walnuts, almonds and hazelnuts. You can add up to 200 g (7 oz) of nuts.*

# Biscuits (cookies),
brownies and bars

# Lavender, honey and almond biscotti thins

*A rustic biscuit (cookie) enriched with elegant flavours of toasted almonds, perfumed honey and dried lavender. Originating from Tuscany, these twice-baked biscuits (cookies), also known as cantucci, are meant to be extra crunchy. Dip them in tea, coffee or Vin Santo, the luscious Italian sweet wine and cantucci's traditional accompaniment.*

*Makes 30–40 biscotti*

**Biscotti**

160 g (5½ oz / 1⅛ cups) almonds, preferably activated dried (see page 25)
110 g (4 oz / ¾ cup) brown rice flour
85 g (3 oz / ⅔ cup) sorghum flour
30 g (1 oz / ¼ cup) arrowroot
3 tsp dried lavender
¼ tsp Himalayan pink salt
2 eggs
70 g (2½ oz / ½ cup plus 1 tbsp) coconut sugar
60 g (2 oz / 3 tbsp) raw honey

**Lavender apricot 'yogurt'**

150 g (5¼ oz / 1⅛ cup) cashew nuts
6 apricots, about 40–50 g (1½–1¾ oz) each
2 tsp lemon juice
¼ vanilla pod (bean), split lengthways and seeds scraped out
10–15 g (⅓–½ oz / ⅔–1 tbsp) blonde coconut nectar or clear raw honey
Generous pinch dried ground lavender

Start by soaking the cashew nuts for the yogurt in 300 ml (10½ fl oz / 1¼ cups) of filtered water and ½ tsp of Himalayan pink salt for 3–4 hours. Drain and rinse thoroughly.

Preheat the oven to 180°C / 350°F / Gas Mark 4. On a baking tray lined with baking parchment, toast the almonds for 6–8 minutes or until they are just taking colour. Leave to cool. Line another tray with baking parchment.

Combine the flours and arrowroot, whisk to disperse any lumps and set aside. In a spice grinder, grind the lavender until it is almost powder. Add to the flours, along with the salt. In a freestanding mixer, whisk the eggs, beginning on a low speed and increasing gradually to high speed, until frothy and as firm as it will get. Pour in the coconut sugar and honey and carry on whipping until just combined and the mix falls in loose ribbons. Remove from the mixer and very lightly fold in the flour mix and almonds until just combined.

On the prepared baking tray, divide the biscotti mix into two logs. The mix will be quite runny so you need to work quickly here. Bake immediately for 10 minutes or until the top is just turning golden and the logs feel soft-firm to touch. Remove from the oven and slice up the logs using a serrated knife, cutting slim biscuits (cookies) no more than 1 cm (⅓ inch) thick. If the logs aren't cutting well, cook for a few more minutes until firmer to cut.

Place the biscuits (cookies) flat on the tray and bake for a further 5–10 minutes, until beginning to take a little colour and firm to touch. Leave to cool. Store in an airtight tin for up to two weeks.

To make the Lavender apricot 'yogurt', remove the stones from the apricots and place in a blender with the soaked cashew nuts, lemon juice, vanilla seeds and sweetener and blend until totally smooth, scraping down and repeating if necessary. Finally add the ground lavender, a small pinch at a time until you reach your preferred flavour. Check the 'yogurt' for sweetness. Pour it into a bowl and serve with the biscuits. Keep in a glass jar in the fridge for about four days.

### NOTES

*A fragrant flower honey, such as lavender honey, is excellent in this recipe.*

*For a truly delicious summer dessert, serve bowlfuls of fresh apricots topped with a spoonful of the velvety apricot-enriched 'yogurt', crumbled biscotti and a drizzle of honey.*

# Rosemary, orange, dark (bittersweet) chocolate and hazelnut sablés

*Literally meaning 'sandy' in French, sablé biscuits (cookies) are delectably buttery, crumbly and just melt in the mouth. While a basic recipe would constitute flour, butter and sugar, here I have added chopped hazelnuts to contrast with the crumbly buckwheat dough, and a marriage of beautiful flavours – rosemary, dark (bittersweet) chocolate and orange.*

**Makes about 14 sablés**

95 g (3¼ oz / ⅓ cup plus 1 tbsp) non-
  hydrogenated dairy-free butter
30 g (1 oz / ¼ cup) coconut sugar
Finely grated zest of ½ orange
2 tsp finely chopped rosemary needles
¼ tsp coarse sea salt, finely ground
1 egg yolk
85 g (3 oz / ⅔ cup) hazelnuts, preferably
  activated dried (see page 25)
65 g (2¼ oz / ⅓ cup plus 2 tbsp)
  buckwheat flour
50 g (1¾ oz) homemade chocolate
  (see page 156) or dark (bittersweet)
  chocolate, 85% cocoa solids

Cream the butter and coconut sugar with the orange zest, chopped rosemary and salt until pale white. Add the egg yolk and carry on mixing. In a food processor, chop the hazelnuts up until quite small but not ground. We want to keep some texture. Combine the nuts with the flour, and add them both to the mix. Finally chop the chocolate into rough pea-sized pieces and add.

The mix will look wet and sticky but this is normal. Scrape the mix out from the mixing bowl onto a 30 cm (12 inch) square piece of baking parchment. Roll out to a log about 4 cm (1½ inches) in diameter, by folding the excess baking parchment over the raw mix and then shaping the mix. Freeze for 2–3 hours (or overnight) until firm enough to cut into discs. You can always re-shape the raw biscuits (cookies) with your hands if necessary.

Preheat the oven to 170°C / 325°F / Gas Mark 3. Line a baking tray with baking parchment.

Cut the dough into 1 cm (⅓ inch) slices, place on the lined tray and bake for 10–15 minutes, rotating the tray halfway, until the edges are dark golden and the centre is coloured too. Baking them properly really brings out the flavour of the nuts and rosemary. Leave to cool completely on the tray and serve. Keeps in a sealed container for up to five days.

**NOTE**
*You could also use dark (bittersweet) chocolate with 75 per cent cocoa solids in this recipe if you find 85 per cent too bitter.*

# Dark (bittersweet) chocolate dipped peanut butter and jelly dreams

*Makes 12 biscuits (cookies)*

**Biscuits (cookies)**

100 g (3½ oz / ⅔ cup) peanuts, preferably activated dried (see page 25)

100 g (3½ oz / ¾ cup plus 1 tbsp) oat flour, plus extra for dusting

4 tsp arrowroot

½ tsp Himalayan pink salt

½ tsp baking powder

40 g (1½ oz / 3 tbsp) coconut oil, softened but not melted

60 g (2 oz / ½ cup) coconut sugar

90 g (3 oz / generous ⅓ cup) smooth peanut butter

1 tsp vanilla extract

300 g (10½ oz) homemade chocolate (see page 156) or dark (bittersweet) chocolate 85% cocoa solids

140 g (5 oz / generous ½ cup) quick-cook raspberry jam (jelly) (see page 32) or no added sugar high fruit content jam (jelly)

**To top**

Maldon or other flaky sea salt

6 freeze-dried raspberries or a small handful of freeze-dried raspberry pieces

*These take the humble peanut butter and jelly sandwich to a whole new level. The dark (bittersweet) chocolate shell cracks to reveal a crumbly and slightly salty peanut butter cookie topped with a layer of sweet yet sharp raspberry jam (jelly) – they are just too good! Dipping the biscuits (cookies) in your homemade chocolate at the end is great fun, and the leftover chocolate... well, I'll leave that up to you!*

Preheat the oven to 170°C / 325°F / Gas Mark 3. Line a baking tray with baking parchment. Blitz the peanuts, oat flour and arrowroot in a food processor until as fine as possible, rocking the food processor gently if necessary. Add the salt and baking powder and blitz once more.

In a large bowl, beat the coconut oil, coconut sugar, peanut butter and vanilla extract using the back of a wooden spoon to get rid of any lumps of coconut oil. Combine the dry ingredients with the coconut and peanut butter mixture. Finish by bringing the mix together with your hands.

Turn the mix out onto a lightly floured surface and roll to just under 1 cm (⅓ inch) thick. Cut out circles using a 6 cm (2½ inch) round cutter. Re-roll and cut again. Transfer onto the lined baking tray, using a knife to scoop them up, and bake for 8 minutes. Rotate the baking tray and bake for a further 8 minutes. The biscuits (cookies) should be light brown. Leave to cool completely on the baking tray. Do not pick them up until they are cold as they are very crumbly and will break easily.

Put a piece of marble or a baking tray lined with baking parchment in the freezer. Melt the chocolate using a bain-marie (see page 156), heating to 28–30°C (82–86°F) for dipping.

With a pastry brush, brush a thin layer of chocolate over the top surface of each cold biscuit (cookie). Leave to dry then spread a layer of jam (jelly) over the chocolate, about 3 mm (⅛ inch) thick.

Remove the cooled marble or baking tray from the freezer. One by one, slide a fork under each biscuit (cookie), and dip it into the chocolate, keeping the fork almost horizontal. Once completely covered, gently tap the fork on the edge of the bowl. Wipe the bottom of the biscuit (cookie) on the side of the bowl, then slide it off the fork onto the marble, using a knife if necessary to push it off.

While the chocolate is still wet, finish each biscuit (cookie) with a sprinkling of sea salt and freeze-dried raspberries, crushed between your fingers. Once set, devour immediately! Or, if you can resist, these will keep in an airtight container for about four days.

# Chilli choc-chip cookies

······································································

*Makes 12 cookies*

1 egg

50 g (1¾ oz / ⅓ cup plus 1 tbsp) coconut
    sugar

130 g (4½ oz / ½ cup) almond butter
    (see page 26)

½ tsp vanilla extract

½ tsp coarse sea salt, ground between
    your fingers

Good few pinches hot chilli powder, or
    more to taste

100 g (3½ oz) homemade chocolate
    (see page 156) or dark (bittersweet)
    chocolate 75–85% cocoa solids,
    depending on your preference,
    chopped into pea-sized chunks

*With their thin crunchy crust and soft chewy centre, these grain-free cookies are irresistible! They are also very quick and easy to make. The hot chilli powder brings a delectably spicy warmth to the palate and pairs beautifully with the bitter dark (bittersweet) chocolate.*

······································································

Preheat the oven to 170°C / 325°F / Gas Mark 3 and line a baking tray with baking parchment. Whisk together the egg and coconut sugar. Add the almond butter and vanilla extract and then the salt. Beat well then mix in the chilli and chocolate. Spoon 1 tablespoon of the mix onto the baking tray at a time, to get 12 cookies in total. Smooth the mounds out with the back of the spoon and your fingers. The cookies should be about 6 cm (2½ inches) in diameter (they don't spread much). Bake for 6 minutes, rotate and bake for a further 3 minutes or until the edges of the cookies are golden brown and the centre feels soft when pressed. Remove from the oven and slide the baking parchment, with the cookies on it, on to a cooling rack. Slide a knife under the cookies to remove them from the paper. They're delicious warm from the oven and get chewier when cooled. Will last for up to five days in an airtight container.

# Chai-spiced oatmeal, raisin, sultana and currant cookies

······································································

*Makes 18–20 cookies*

105 g (3¾ oz / 1⅛ cups) gluten-free
    rolled oats, plus extra for sprinkling

45 g (1½ oz / generous ⅓ cup) oat flour

45 g (1½ oz / ⅓ cup plus 1 tbsp) gram
    flour

25 g (¾ oz / 3 tbsp) cornflour
    (cornstarch)

25 g (¾ oz / 3 tbsp) arrowroot

25 g (¾ oz / ¼ cup) milled flax seeds

¾ tsp bicarbonate of soda (baking soda)

1 tsp Himalayan pink salt

105 g (3¾ oz / ⅔ cup) Palmyra nectar
    powder

½ tsp ground ginger

½ tsp ground cloves

½ tsp ground cardamom

1½ tsp ground cinnamon

Pinch black pepper, optional

¾ tsp guar gum

40 g (1½ oz / ¼ cup) currants

40 g (1½ oz / ¼ cup) sultanas (seedless
    golden raisins)

40 g (1½ oz / ¼ cup) raisins

150 ml (5 fl oz / scant ⅔ cup) EVCP
    rapeseed oil

125 g (4½ oz / ½ cup) easy apple purée
    (see page 32)

2 tsp vanilla extract

*I have always loved oatmeal and raisin cookies, so I have to be very strong-willed when I bake a batch of these! When cooked, the edges become slightly crunchy and chewy while the middle stays sublimely soft, studded with juicy dried fruit. The spices add their sweet warming flavours, making it hard to resist another one!*

······································································

Preheat the oven to 170°C / 325°F / Gas Mark 3 and line a large baking tray with baking parchment.

Combine all the dry ingredients from the rolled oats to the guar gum. Using a whisk, mix them together well, making sure the guar gum is well dispersed. Add the currants, sultanas (seedless golden raisins) and raisins. Make a well in the centre of the dry mix and add the oil, apple purée and vanilla extract and mix with a wooden spoon. Weigh out 40 g (1½ oz) of cookie dough to make one cookie, then use this as a size guide; or divide the dough to make 18–20 cookies. Using a dessert spoon, spoon out blobs about the same size as the guide onto the tray, slightly flattening them with the back of the spoon and your fingers. You'll get a bit sticky here. You want the cookies to be just over 1 cm (⅓ inch) thick. Sprinkle the cookies with the extra oats.

Bake for 7 minutes, rotate the tray and cook for 2–3 more minutes, until the cookies are golden brown, the edges are slightly darker and just hard, while the centre is still soft to touch. Leave to cool on a rack for 10 minutes, then enjoy while warm. The cookies will keep for at least three days in an airtight container and freeze well too.

# Tutti frutti buckwheat florentines

......................................................................................

**Makes about 20 florentines**

100 g (3½ oz / ⅔ cup) almonds,
preferably activated dried (see page
25), roughly chopped

100 g (3½ oz / ⅔ cup) buckwheat
groats, preferably activated dried
(see page 25)

40 g (1½ oz / ¼ cup) dried unsulphured
apricots, chopped into small pieces

40 g (1½ oz / ¼ cup) dried unsweetened
blueberries

40 g (1½ oz / ⅓ cup) dried cranberries

30 g (1 oz / generous 2 tbsp) coconut oil

50 g (1¾ oz / ⅓ cup plus 1 tbsp) coconut
sugar

20 g (¾ oz / 1⅓ tbsp) coconut nectar

20 g (¾ oz / scant 3 tbsp) buckwheat
flour

150 ml (5 fl oz / scant ⅔ cup) coconut
milk

200 g (7 oz) homemade chocolate
(see page 156) or dark (bittersweet)
chocolate 85% cocoa solids

*Extremely quick to rustle up, these are yummy, chewy, crunchy, nutty, fruity
sensations! Play around with the fruits and nuts. I love the tart sweet cranberries,
blueberries and apricots with almonds, but currants, chopped figs, hazelnuts and
pistachio nuts all work well.*

......................................................................................

Preheat the oven to 170°C / 325°F / Gas Mark 3 and line one large baking tray with
a silicone mat or baking parchment.

Mix together the chopped almonds and buckwheat groats with the apricots,
blueberries and cranberries, pulling apart any large clumps of dried fruit with
your fingertips.

In a small–medium saucepan, melt the oil with the coconut sugar and nectar,
being careful not to let it catch. Add the flour, whisking for almost a minute
to make a thick paste, then immediately add the coconut milk, whisking
continuously until smooth and thick, no longer than one more minute.

Remove the saucepan from the heat and stir in the nut and fruit mix. Spoon out
heaped teaspoons of the mix onto the prepared tray, leaving about 1 cm (⅓ inch)
between each mound. Flatten each mound slightly with the back of a spoon. Bake
for 10 minutes, rotate the tray and bake for about another 5 minutes. The tops of
the biscuits (cookies) should be golden brown. Remove from the oven and leave
to cool completely on the tray.

Melt the chocolate slowly in a bain-marie (see page 156), heating to 28–30°C
(82–86°F) for dipping.  When the florentines are cold, dip the base of each one in
the chocolate, dropping it in and then scooping it out with a fork. Shake off any
excess chocolate, wipe the bottom of the biscuit (cookie) on the side of the bowl,
and put the biscuits (cookies), with the chocolate facing upwards, onto a piece of
baking parchment. If you want, mark the chocolate bottom using a fork, using a
zig-zag movement to go across the chocolate before it sets. Leave in a cool place
or refrigerate for a few minutes to set. Serve immediately.

Keep in a sealed container for up to five days.

# Waste not, want not raw herby hemp seed crackers

........................................................................................

*Made with vegetable juice pulp and nut milk pulp, these tasty crackers work well with hummus, baba ghanoush and other dips, or break them up and sprinkle onto salads. The oniony chives, parsley and basil marry well with the fresh flavours of the vegetables and lime, while the chilli and za'atar add extra depth.*

........................................................................................

*Juice serves 1*
*Makes about 90 crackers*

**Super alkaline green juice**
*Makes about 170 g (6 oz/compact 1¼ cups) juice pulp*
80 g (2¾ oz) kale (a generous handful)
25 g (¾ oz) spinach (a small handful)
⅓ cucumber (about 135 g/4¾ oz)
2–3 celery stalks (about 115 g/4 oz)
20 g (¾ oz/⅓ cup) flat-leaf or curly parsley (a small handful)
1 small pear (about 120 g/4¼ oz)

**Crackers**
170 g (6 oz/compact 1¼ cups) juice pulp (see above)
200 g (7 oz/compact 1⅛ cups) almond or hazelnut milk pulp, from 1 x recipe nut milk (see page 28)
120 g (4¼ oz/scant ½ cup) tahini, preferably raw
100 g (3½ oz/generous ¾ cup) shelled hemp seeds, plus extra for sprinkling
45 g (1½ oz/scant 1 cup) chives, finely chopped
45 g (1½ oz/⅔ cup) parsley (without stalks), finely chopped
20 g (¾ oz/scant 1 cup) basil, finely chopped
1–1½ tsp Himalayan pink salt
Black pepper to taste
2 tbsp psyllium husk powder
Finely grated zest and 20 ml (¾ fl oz/ 4 tsp) juice of 1 lime
Tiny pinch chilli flakes, optional
½ tsp za'atar, optional

Put all the ingredients for the crackers into a large bowl and mix with your hands, squeezing the mix through your fingers until you get a doughy, herby ball. Check and adjust the seasoning as necessary.

Spread a piece of the mix out thinly on a piece of baking parchment or a silicone mat (or whatever you use in your dehydrator). Start off using your hands to spread it, dipping your fingers into water then pressing out the mix. Next use a knife, preferably a step palette knife (frosting spatula), to spread the mix very thinly to 3–4 mm (⅛ inch) thick and no thicker than 5 mm (⅓ inch). If the mix feels too stiff to spread, dip the knife into water too, which will help the mix spread more easily and evenly.

With a knife, mark the crackers into squares or rectangles – I like 5 x 4 cm (2 x 1½ inch) rectangles. Sprinkle with extra hemp seeds, pressing them in slightly, if desired. Repeat the whole process using more baking parchment or silicone mats, until all of the dough has been spread.

Place in the dehydrator and dehydrate for 24 hours at 45°C/113°F. I like them to be crisp but with a little chew, but dry them out for longer if you want them crunchier. If you do not have a dehydrator, just set your oven to the lowest temperature and take that into account with the timing. As a guide, my oven's lowest temperature is 60°C (140°F) and the crackers take about 3–4 hours to cook, but they will be golden-brown rather than green.

The crackers will keep for up to two weeks in a sealed container. Store in the fridge for extra freshness.

### NOTE
*The juice and pulp I have used is just a guide. All you need is the fibre and moisture from the pulp to make these, so don't worry if you have slightly different amounts of pulp or have made a different juice, just adjust the other ingredients accordingly and taste the mix as you go. Add your own favourite herbs and spices and play around with flavours. Ground turmeric, ginger and cumin work well with celery, beetroot, carrot, fresh ginger and apple juice as seen in the orangey coloured crackers (shown opposite).*

# Chocolate truffle teff brownies

*Makes 30 rectangles or 48 triangles*

100 g (3½ oz / ½ cup) coconut oil
150 g (5¼ oz) dark (bittersweet)
  chocolate, 100% cocoa solids
280 g (10 oz / 2¼ cups) coconut sugar
1 tsp coarse sea salt, plus ½ tsp extra for
  sprinkling
4 eggs
2 tsp vanilla extract
80 g (2¾ oz / generous ½ cup) teff flour

*Nestled in the cloud forest of the Andes, I tasted the best brownies ever at El Quetzal de Mindo in Ecuador. The secret of their mind-blowing intensity was a special ingredient – 100 per cent cacao liquor, made from beans from the plantation where the brownies were baked. I have tried my hardest to recreate them here...*

Preheat the oven to 170°C / 325°F / Gas Mark 3. Grease and line a 30 x 20 x 2 cm deep (12 x 8 x ¾ inch) brownie tin.

Melt the oil with the chocolate in a bain-marie (see page 156). Once melted, remove from the heat and mix in the sugar and salt, grinding it between your fingers, followed by the eggs and vanilla extract. Finally mix in the flour until just combined. The mix should look smooth and glossy. Pour into the prepared tin. Sprinkle with the extra salt and bake for 15 minutes, rotating the tin after 10 minutes, until a skewer inserted in the centre comes out just clean. The brownies should feel firm to touch and will be cracking slightly around the edges.

Leave to cool completely in the tin then cut into 30 rectangles, each 5 x 4 cm (2 x 1½ inch), or make 48 small triangles, by cutting 5 cm (2 inch) squares diagonally in half. As the brownies are very rich, for me a small triangle will suffice. They are also great served as petit fours or with the Velvet chocolate pots on page 141. These brownies will keep for up to five days in the fridge or are suitable for freezing. They're even yummy eaten straight from frozen.

# Sour cherry and macadamia butterscotch blondies

*Makes 20 blondies*

2 eggs
100 g (3½ oz / ¾ cup plus 1 tbsp) coconut
  sugar, plus extra for sprinkling
260 g (9¼ oz / 1 cup) cashew butter (see
  page 26)
1 tsp coarse sea salt
1 vanilla pod (bean), split lengthways
  and seeds scraped out
Finely grated zest of 1 small lemon
40 g (1½ oz / scant 3 tbsp) cacao butter
60 g (2 oz / generous ⅓ cup) dried sour
  cherries
70 g (2½ oz / ½ cup) macadamia nut
  halves
1 tsp baking powder
40 g (1½ oz / ⅓ cup) ground almonds
  (almond meal)

*The chewy sour cherries really make these grain-free blondies. Their sweet sharpness cuts through the butterscotch and white chocolate-like flavours created by the mixture of cacao and cashew butters, coconut sugar and creamy crunchy macadamia nuts, all these components melting deliciously together with each bite.*

Preheat the oven to 160°C / 310°F / Gas Mark 2½ and grease and line a 20 cm (8 inch) square brownie tin with baking parchment.

Mix the eggs with the coconut sugar. Combine the cashew butter, salt, vanilla seeds and lemon zest and beat it into the egg mix, stirring well. Melt the cacao butter and add to the mix along with 40 g (1½ oz / ¼ cup) of the sour cherries and half the macadamia nuts. Finally combine the baking powder and ground almonds (almond meal) and fold them into the mix. Pour into the prepared tin and top with the remaining sour cherries and macadamia nuts, pressing them into the mix well. Sprinkle with a good handful of coconut sugar to cover.

Bake for 20–25 minutes, turning the tray halfway, until the top is golden brown and just starting to crack and the edges are slightly darker. Leave to cool before cutting. These will keep for five days in an airtight container and freeze well too.

# Salted tahini shortbread biscuit (cookie) bars with yogurt-coated walnuts and figs

*These bars are crazy-good! Crunchy toasted walnuts and sweet, juicy dried figs coated in homemade yogurt-like 'white chocolate' on a slightly salty buttery biscuit (cookie) base, what more could you want? For it to be guilt-free, too? Well, here you are! Hard to put down and devilishly moreish, these won't be around for long.*

*Makes 24 square bars*

**'White chocolate yogurt'**

120 g (4¼ oz / scant ½ cup) cashew butter (see page 26)

180 g (6¼ oz / ¾ cup plus 1 tbsp) cacao butter, melted

½ vanilla pod (bean), split lengthways and seeds scraped out

Finely grated zest of ½ lemon

65 g (2¼ oz / generous 3 tbsp) raw honey

Pinch Himalyan pink salt

**Biscuit (cookie)**

360 g (12¾ oz / 3½ cups) walnuts, preferably activated dried (see page 25)

80 g (2¾ oz / ⅓ cup plus 1 tbsp) coconut oil, softened but not melted

120 g (4¼ oz / scant 1 cup) coconut sugar

180 g (6¼ oz / ¾ cup) light tahini

2 tsp vanilla extract

200 g (7 oz / 1⅔ cups) oat flour

20 g (¾ oz / 2½ tbsp) arrowroot

2 tsp coarse sea salt, finely ground

1 tsp baking powder

200 g (7 oz / 1¼ cups) dried figs, small stalks removed

To make the 'white chocolate yogurt' place everything in a blender and blend until completely smooth. Pour into a bowl and set aside, leaving it in a warm place so it does not set.

Preheat the oven to 170°C / 325°F / Gas Mark 3. Line a 30 x 20 x 3 cm deep (12 x 8 x 1¼ inch) tin with baking parchment. Line another tray with baking parchment and toast 160 g (5½ oz / 1½ cups) of the walnuts on it for 7 minutes or until just beginning to colour. Set aside to cool.

Beat together the coconut oil, coconut sugar, tahini and vanilla extract until smooth.

Blitz the remaining 200 g (7 oz / 2 cups) of walnuts in a food processor with the oat flour and arrowroot until as fine as possible. Add the salt and baking powder and blitz once more. Combine the dry ingredients with the tahini, sugar and oil mixture. Finish by bringing the mix together with your hands. Press the biscuit (cookie) mix into the prepared tin, smoothing it out to make an even base with a step palette knife (frosting spatula). Bake for 30–35 minutes, turning halfway, until light brown. Leave to cool.

Roughly chop the figs into about 4–6 pieces each. Roughly chop the toasted walnuts into pieces a bit larger than peas. Mix thoroughly into the 'white chocolate yogurt' and then immediately pour over the cooled tahini shortbread base. Leave to set in the freezer for 30 minutes, then remove from the tin and cut with a large serrated knife into 5 cm (2 inch) squares and serve.

Keeps well for five days in a sealed container.

### NOTE
*For a vegan 'white chocolate yogurt', blonde coconut nectar works well in the place of the raw honey.*

# Raw super seed energy boosters

*Containing the kings of the seeds: hemp, flax, chia and pumpkin, these bars certainly deliver on nutrition, being power-packed with protein, essential fatty acids and fibre. I also like to add the superfood moringa, which has 13 essential vitamins and minerals, is high in protein and rich in iron and antioxidants.*

*Makes 25 squares*

150 g (5¼ oz / 1 cup) dried figs, hard stalks removed

Grated zest and 70 ml (2½ fl oz / ¼ cup plus 2 tsp) juice of 1 orange

1 tbsp cold pressed flax seed oil

30 g (1 oz / 2 tbsp) tahini, raw if possible

2 tsp vanilla extract

½ tsp Himalayan pink salt

2 tbsp chia seeds

5 tbsp pumpkin seeds, preferably activated dried (see page 25)

5 tbsp hulled hemp seeds

100 g (3½ oz / ½ cup) Brazil nuts, roughly chopped into about 3 pieces

2 tbsp hemp protein powder

1–2 tsp moringa powder, optional

100 g (3½ oz / ⅔ cup) almonds, preferably activated dried (see page 25)

20 g (¾ oz / 3 tbsp) goji berries

Line a 20 cm (8 inch) square tin with baking parchment.

Process the figs in a food processor with the orange zest and juice, oil, tahini, vanilla extract and salt, stopping the mixer and scraping down until a roughly smooth paste forms. Add the rest of the ingredients, except the almonds and goji berries, and process until it forms a ball-like paste. Finally add the almonds and goji berries, pulsing a few times just to cut up some of the almonds. Most of the almonds should stay whole, which adds a nice crunch to the soft bars.

Press the mix into the prepared tin, spreading it out evenly. Refrigerate for about 1 hour and then cut up into 4 cm (1½ inch) squares and enjoy from the fridge or freezer. If you prefer, you can make the squares into balls instead. They keep for at least five days in the fridge, or freeze well for at least a month.

# Almond, oat and raspberry bars

*These are great for breakfast on the go, children's snacks, picnics or to combat that mid-afternoon energy-slump. Fruity, crumbly, moist and moreish, they're far better than a bog standard fruit square any day!*

*Makes 12 slices or 24 small squares*

120 g (4¼ oz / 1 cup) oat flour

100 g (3½ oz / 1 cup plus 2 tbsp) gluten-free rolled oats, plus 20 g (¾ oz / scant ¼ cup) for topping

1 tsp ground cinnamon

3 tsp arrowroot

1 tsp baking powder

1 tsp Himalayan pink salt

120 g (4¼ oz / scant ½ cup) almond butter (see page 26)

1 vanilla pod (bean), split lengthways and seeds scraped out

100 g (3½ oz / scant ½ cup) coconut nectar, plus 1 tbsp extra

Finely grated zest of 1 lemon

200 g (7 oz / 1⅔ cups) raspberries, fresh or frozen

120 g (4¼ oz / ½ cup) easy apple purée (see page 32)

50 g (1¾ oz / generous ½ cup) flaked almonds

Preheat the oven to 160°C / 310°F / Gas Mark 2½ and line a 20 x 20 x 3 cm deep (8 x 8 x 1¼ inch) tray with baking parchment.

Combine all the dry ingredients. In a large bowl, mix the almond butter with the vanilla seeds, 100 g (3½ oz / scant ½ cup) coconut nectar and lemon zest. Add the dry ingredients to the almond butter mix and stir together. The mix will be quite stiff so use your hands to combine it if necessary. Weigh the mix and put three-quarters of it into the base of the tin, pushing it into the corners and flattening it to make a ½ cm (⅕ inch) thick base.

Mash together the raspberries, apple purée and 1 tbsp of coconut nectar using a fork and pour onto the base. Crumble up the remainder of the oat mix and add in the flaked almonds and extra oats. Crumble this mix over the fruit and really press it into the fruit, otherwise it will all just crumble off when eating. Bake for 15 minutes. Open the oven and, wearing oven gloves, lightly press the semi-baked crumble mix into the fruit, then bake for a further 10–15 minutes until the crumble and almond top is golden brown and the edges look dark golden.

Leave to cool completely in the tin and then slice up into 12 pieces, each 8 x 4 cm (3 x 1½ inches), or cut in half for 24 smaller squares. They keep for five days in an airtight container in the fridge and freeze well too.

# Five grain omega mix granola bars

**Makes about 30 bars**

100 g (3½ oz / scant 1 cup) walnuts, roughly chopped

50 g (1¾ oz / scant ⅓ cup) flax seeds

50 g (1¾ oz / generous ⅓ cup) sesame seeds

100 g (3½ oz / generous ⅔ cup) sunflower seeds

100 g (3½ oz / ⅔ cup) pumpkin seeds

80 g (2¾ oz / scant 1 cup) gluten-free oats

80 g (2¾ oz / ¾ cup) buckwheat flakes

80 g (2¾ oz / ¾ cup) quinoa flakes

80 g (2¾ oz / ¾ cup) brown rice flakes

80 g (2¾ oz / ¾ cup) millet flakes

50 g (1¾ oz / scant ½ cup) milled flax seeds

1 tsp mixed spice

1 tsp ground cinnamon

1½ tsp coarse sea salt, ground

2 tsp vanilla extract

200 g (7 oz / ¾ cup plus 1 tbsp) easy apple purée (see page 32)

150 ml (5 fl oz / scant ⅔ cup) EVCP rapeseed oil

Zest and juice of 1 orange

*Wholegrains are great, especially when used in combination, each having its own dietary attributes and creating a fuelling complex carbohydrate blend. Adding a balanced mix of seeds and walnuts to supply you and your family with a good dose of your daily omega 3 and 6 intake, these bars are pretty awesome.*

Soak the walnuts and all the seeds, except the milled flax seeds, for 8 hours or overnight in 1 litre (35 fl oz / 4¼ cups) of filtered water with 2 tsp of Himalayan pink salt (see also page 25). Drain and rinse thoroughly.

Preheat the oven to 160°C / 310°F / Gas Mark 2½. Line a 30 x 20 x 3 cm deep (12 x 8 x 1¼ inch) tray with baking parchment.

In a large bowl, combine the oats, all the flakes, milled flax seeds, mixed spice, cinnamon and salt. Add the soaked nuts and seeds and combine. Combine the vanilla, apple purée, oil and orange zest and juice, then pour over the dry ingredients and mix well.

Put all the mix into the prepared tray, pressing it down really well into the corners and compacting it. Cook for 1 hour, turning the tray halfway, until the top is golden brown and firm to touch, while the edges are slightly darker. Leave to cool completely in the tin. Lift out of the tin onto a chopping board and cut into 2.5 x 6.5 cm (1 x 2½ inch) bars, using a sharp serrated knife.

Increase the oven temperature to 170°C / 325°F / Gas Mark 3. Bake the sliced bars on a baking tray lined with parchment for a further 20–25 minutes, turning the bars over halfway through baking to give both sides a golden colour. They keep for up to five days in a sealed container and freeze well too.

**VARIATIONS**

*Naturally sweetened five grain omega mix granola bars*
I like to keep these bars sugar-free to highlight the great flavours of the toasted seeds, nuts and grains, but if you prefer them sweeter then add 5 tbsp of date syrup, or your preferred natural liquid sweetener, and 150 g (5¼ oz / 1 cup) dates chopped into small pea-size pieces, or another dried fruit, when you add the orange zest and juice.

*Hazelnut, buckwheat and blueberry bars*
Follow the recipe for Almond, oat and raspberry bars, but replace the oat flour and flakes with buckwheat flour and flakes; almond butter with hazelnut butter; flaked almonds with chopped hazelnuts; and raspberries with blueberries.

*Previous spread: Top left, Five grain omega mix granola bars; bottom left, Almond, oat and raspberry bars; top right, Almond, oat and raspberry bars; centre right, Hazelnut, buckwheat and blueberry bars; bottom right, Raw super seed energy boosters.*

# Coconut-cacao-quinoa bars

*Makes 12 bars*

**Bars**

120 g (4¼ oz / ¾ cup) pitted Medjool
   dates
1 vanilla pod (bean), cut lengthways
   and seeds scraped out
1 tsp vanilla extract
1 tsp Himalayan pink salt
1¼ tsp ground cinnamon
50 g (1¾ oz) homemade chocolate
   (see page 156) or dark (bittersweet)
   chocolate 85% cocoa solids
100 g (3½ oz / 1¼ cups) desiccated
   coconut
50 g (1¾ oz / ½ cup) quinoa flakes
50 g (1¾ oz / scant ½ cup) cacao nibs
60 g (2 oz / generous ¼ cup) coconut oil
20 g (¾ oz / 1⅓ tbsp) coconut nectar

**To top**

100 g (3½ oz) homemade chocolate
   (see page 156) or dark (bittersweet)
   chocolate 85% cocoa solids
20 g (¾ oz / ¼ cup) desiccated coconut

*If you like dark (bittersweet) chocolate and coconut (and let's face it, who doesn't?), then watch out as these are seriously scrummy! With a hint of Himalayan pink salt and vanilla to enliven them, this is a flavour combination that never fails. Packed with goodness, these are easy to make, so get prepared and bake a batch to have for the week ahead.*

Grease and line an 18 x 11 x 8 cm deep (7 x 4¼ x 3 inch) loaf tin with baking parchment, making sure that the parchment comes up around the edges.

Put the dates in a food processor with the vanilla seeds and extract, salt and cinnamon and blend to a rough paste. Roughly chop the chocolate into small pieces, add it to the dates, along with the desiccated coconut, quinoa flakes and cacao nibs, and blend. Melt the coconut oil, add to the date mix with the coconut nectar and blend once more until the mix is well combined. A piece of the mix flattened in your hand will stick together.

Remove the mix from the food processor and press well into the prepared tin. Smooth out the top using your hands and a step palette knife (frosting spatula), and freeze for 1 hour.

Remove the set mix from the tin. Cut into 12 bars, just under 1.5 cm (½ inch) wide, using a serrated knife. Put the desiccated coconut for the topping on to a deep plate or bowl. Melt the chocolate for the topping in a bain-marie (see page 156). You will need to use a bowl that is deep enough to fit the bars in so that the chocolate covers a bit more than 1 cm (⅓ inch) of their depth, but also large enough to fit the 11 cm (4¼ inch) bars.

When the chocolate is around 28–30°C (82–86°F), dip in the bars lengthways, one by one, so the bottom half of the bar is coated in chocolate. Shake off the excess chocolate, wipe the bar on the side of the bowl, then dip the bottom of the bar into the coconut while the chocolate is still wet. Leave on a tray to set, with the coconut layer facing upwards.

When all the bars have been dipped in the chocolate, pour any leftover chocolate onto a piece of baking parchment, refrigerate it, and, when set, snap up and store in a glass jar in the fridge.

Store the bars in the fridge where they will keep well for five days, or freeze. Eat them at their best, cold, straight from the fridge or freezer. I also love crumbling them over coconut yogurt.

*NOTE*
*I like to dip the bars in chocolate as it makes an impressive and tasty finish, but this stage can be skipped if you prefer, and the bars will still taste great.*

# Gorgeous tarts and scrumptious pies

# Blueberry galettes

........................................................................................

**Makes 6 galettes**

480 g (1 lb 1 oz/3 cups) blueberries,
  fresh or frozen
2 tbsp lemon juice
2 tbsp coconut sugar, plus 15 g (½ oz/
  1½ tbsp), and extra for topping
15 g (½ oz/2½ tbsp) ground almonds
  (almond meal)
15 g (½ oz/1¾ tbsp) almonds,
  preferably activated dried (see page
  25), roughly chopped
1 tsp ground cinnamon
¼ tsp Himalayan pink salt
360 g (12¾ oz) basic pastry (see page 30)

*The blueberries are the stars of these simple but delicious tarts so I highly recommend that you find the best quality blueberries, preferably local or organic. It really pays off as the ones in supermarkets often lack flavour. Sweet cherries, when in season, make an ideal substitute for blueberries.*

........................................................................................

Preheat the oven to 170°C/325°2F/Gas Mark 3. Line a large baking tray with baking parchment.

In a large bowl, mix together the blueberries (allow to thaw slightly first if using frozen) with the lemon juice and 2 tbsp coconut sugar. Leave for 30 minutes to macerate. Mix together the ground and chopped almonds with the 15 g (½ oz/ 1½ tbsp) coconut sugar, cinnamon and salt.

Roll out the pastry to about 3 mm (⅛ inch) thick. Using a large cookie cutter or a small plate with a 13 cm (5 inch) diameter, cut out 6 circles of pastry (each circle should weigh around 60 g (2 oz)), rerolling as necessary. As you cut each one, put it onto the lined baking tray, leaving at least 2.5 cm (1 inch) between each disc.

Divide the almond mix between the 6 discs, placing it in the centre and leaving about 2 cm (¾ inch) around the edges. Top the almond mix with the blueberries, keeping the mixture in the centre of the discs. Reserve the macerating juices.

Next, turn the pastry up around the berries; work as if you are building walls of pastry around them. The pastry might break so this part requires patience. Fold up the pastry with your fingertips or carefully slip a knife under each section of pastry, working around in a circle. Once all the edges are up, seal any holes and smooth out the edges using the back of a kitchen knife and your fingertips. Don't worry about over-working the pastry, there's no gluten in it to work!

Finish by pouring the leftover juices onto the berries and sprinkle each galette with a generous pinch of coconut sugar. Bake for about 15 minutes, rotating the tray halfway through the cooking time. The galettes are ready when the fruit juices are bubbling and the pastry is golden brown.

Leave to cool on the baking tray before moving the galettes carefully with a large spatula as they are fragile and will collapse if moved while too hot. These are best served fresh, ideally slightly warm from the oven, but will still be good for up to three days.

**NOTE**
*If you want to make one large galette instead of the six smaller ones, roll the pastry out into a large circle and double the cooking time to 30 minutes.*

# Plum crostata

*Serves 12–16*

**Plum crostata**

Coconut oil, for greasing

500 g (1 lb 2 oz) basic pastry (see page
30), rolled to about 3 mm (⅛ inch)
thick

About 30 fresh firm plums

2 tbsp raw honey

**Plum jam (jelly)**

20 de-stoned plums, about 600 g
(1 lb 5 oz) de-stoned weight, fresh
or frozen

300 g (10½ oz / 1¼ cups) easy apple
purée (see page 32)

60 g (2 oz / ½ cup) coconut sugar

*Every summer we just cannot get enough of the succulent plums in our garden, so
this recipe is dedicated to the annual British plum glut! It is simple to make, so pretty
in appearance and at once sweet, tart and fresh. Add a dollop of vanilla ice cream and
you're away!*

Preheat the oven to 170°C / 325°F / Gas Mark 3. Grease a round 28 x 4 cm deep
(11 x 1½ inch) tart tin with coconut oil. Line the tin with the pastry then blind
bake (see page 31) for 15 minutes until the edges are golden brown. Remove the
lining and baking beans and bake for a further 10–20 minutes or until the base
of the pastry is turning golden brown and the edges are slightly darker. Set aside
to cool.

To make the plum jam (jelly), put all the jam (jelly) ingredients into a medium–
large saucepan. Bring to the boil, lower the heat slightly and cook for about
5 minutes, breaking up the plums with a spoon. Turn down to a simmer and
continue to cook the mix, stirring occasionally, until it has reduced to a thick and
relatively smooth jam (jelly). Remove from the heat.

While the jam (jelly) cooks, halve the plums and remove the stones. Fill the
cooked pastry base evenly with the jam (jelly) and then top with the halved
plums, placed vertically into the jam (jelly), starting at the edge of the tart and
working inwards. Drizzle with the honey and bake for about 20 minutes until the
plums are just softening. The filling will be very juicy, but this is normal.

This tart is best eaten fresh on the day it is baked, or for breakfast the next
morning.

### NOTES

*I love the tartness of the fresh plums on top of the sweet jam (jelly) and pastry, but you
can drizzle the baked tart with an additional 1–2 tbsp of raw honey if you prefer a sweeter
finish, or serve the tart with extra honey if you like.*

*If you are vegan, replace the honey with coconut nectar or your preferred vegan sweetener.*

# Raspberry and rose tartlets with pistachio frangipane

.....................................................................

*I look forward to autumn raspberries every year, they're just so plump and juicy! They form the sweet centres of these divine vegan morsels (summer raspberries work too), surrounded by a soft but crunchy pistachio frangipane, all encased in crumbly buckwheat and almond pastry. I don't think they could be any more heavenly.*

.....................................................................

**Makes 12 tartlets**

70 g (2½ oz / ½ cup) pistachio nuts, preferably activated dried (see page 25)

1 tbsp milled flax seeds

3 tbsp filtered water

20 g (¾ oz / 3 tbsp) ground almonds (almond meal)

30 g (1 oz / ¼ cup) coconut sugar

¼ tsp Himalayan pink salt

Finely grated zest of ¼ lemon

45 g (1½ oz / 3½ tbsp) coconut oil, plus extra for greasing

10 g (⅓ oz / ½ tbsp) raw pistachio paste, optional

200 g (7 oz) basic pastry (see page 30), rolled out to about 3 mm (⅛ inch) thick

6 tsp quick-cook raspberry jam (jelly) (see page 32), or no added sugar high fruit content raspberry jam (jelly)

150–200 g (5–7 oz / scant 1¼–1⅔ cups) fresh or frozen raspberries

½–1 tbsp rosewater for brushing, plus 1½ tsp for glazing

3 tsp no added sugar high fruit content apricot jam (jelly)

**To decorate**
Fresh rose petals
Chopped pistachio nuts

Preheat the oven to 170°C / 325°F / Gas Mark 3. Grease a 12-hole tartlet tin with a little coconut oil. On a baking tray lined with baking parchment, toast the pistachio nuts for 5–7 minutes until just beginning to colour. Set aside to cool.

Mix the milled flax seeds with the measured water and leave for about 15 minutes to form a thick gel. Blitz the cooled pistachio nuts in a food processor fitted with a blade. Do not grind them down completely; some should be finely ground while the rest are in slightly larger pieces for texture.

To make the frangipane, combine the semi-ground pistachio nuts with the ground almonds (almond meal), coconut sugar, salt and lemon zest. Melt the coconut oil and add it to the dry ingredients along with the raw pistachio paste, if using. Finally fold in the flax seed gel. Set the mix aside.

Using a 6 cm (2½ inch) fluted cookie cutter, cut out 12 pastry rounds and place them in the moulds, making sure there are no air gaps. Cover the bottom of each pastry case with about ¼–½ tsp of raspberry jam (jelly). Divide the frangipane between the 12 tartlets, covering the layer of jam (jelly). You will get about 1 tbsp of frangipane per tartlet. Top each tartlet with 2–3 raspberries, depending on their size. Some autumn raspberries are huge! Slightly push them into the frangipane.

Bake for 10 minutes, turn and bake for another 2–4 minutes. They are ready when the frangipane is slightly bubbling and the edges of the pastry shells are golden brown, as is the outside of the frangipane. Leave to cool for 10 minutes, then, while the tartlets are still warm, brush with rosewater. I recommend using ½–1 tbsp in total for all 12, brushed on with a pastry brush and left to sink in. For each tartlet, immerse the pastry brush in the rosewater and brush generously over.

To make the glaze, mix the apricot jam (jelly) with 1½ tsp of rosewater. When the tartlets are completely cool, glaze them using a pastry brush. Using a small palette knife (frosting spatula) or kitchen knife, remove each tartlet from the mould and serve, finishing off with chopped pistachio nuts and fresh rose petals. Serve for afternoon tea, or for pudding with clouds of whipped vanilla coconut cream (see page 27). These will last well in a sealed container for at least three days.

**NOTES**

*Tartlet tins vary in size so you may need to use a different sized cutter for the pastry, depending on the size of your tin. Leftover pastry can be baked off as biscuits (cookies) or frozen.*

*Rosewaters greatly vary in strength and flavour so try to seek out a more delicate one. I love Steenbergs organic rosewater (see Stockists on page 176).*

# Pear, chocolate and hazelnut tart with cacao pastry crust

....................................................................................

*This pudding is inspired by two classics, Poires Belle Hélène, poached pears with chocolate sauce, and Tarte Bourdaloue, pâte sucrée filled with pear and almond frangipane. In this wonderfully textured tart, a crunchy cacao crust surrounds a gooey centre of soft, sweet pears, immersed in a chocolate and hazelnut frangipane.*

....................................................................................

*Serves 8–10*

### Cacao pastry crust

45 g (1½ oz / 3½ tbsp) coconut oil, plus extra for greasing
75 g (2¾ oz / ⅔ cup) ground hazelnuts
60 g (2 oz / ⅓ cup plus 1 tbsp) buckwheat flour, plus extra for dusting
15 g (½ oz / 3 tbsp) cacao powder
30 g (1 oz / ¼ cup) coconut sugar
10 g (⅓ oz / 1¼ tbsp) arrowroot
¼ tsp Himalayan pink salt
35 ml (1¼ fl oz / 7 tsp) water

### Chocolate and hazelnut frangipane

3 tbsp milled flax seeds
9 tbsp water
200 g (7 oz / 1½ cups) hazelnuts, preferably activated dried (see page 25)
20 g (¾ oz / 3 tbsp) ground hazelnuts or ground almonds (almond meal)
20 g (¾ oz / 4 tbsp) cacao powder
½ tsp Himalayan pink salt
90 g (3 oz) homemade chocolate (see page 156) or dark (bittersweet) chocolate 85% cocoa solids, roughly chopped into pea-size pieces
130 g (4½ oz / scant ⅔ cup) coconut oil, melted
120 g (4¼ oz / generous ⅓ cup) raw honey
30 g (1 oz / 2 tbsp) hazelnut butter (see page 26) (or almond butter (see page 26))
4 medium-large sweet pears, just under 1 kg (2 lbs 3 oz), preferably Comice, ripe but still quite firm

### Glaze

2–3 tbsp no added sugar high fruit content apricot jam (jelly)

Grease a 33 x 12.5 cm (13 x 5 inch) rectangular tart tin or a 23 cm (9 inch) round tart tin with coconut oil. Line a baking tray with baking parchment. For the pastry, melt the measured coconut oil and set aside. Mix together the dry ingredients with a whisk to disperse any lumps. Pour in the coconut oil then the water and stir until well combined.

Spread out a piece of baking parchment slightly larger than the tart tin and lightly dust with buckwheat flour. Place the pastry on the parchment and pat it out to about the size of the tart tin. Lightly dust the surface with more flour, cover with another layer of parchment and roll it out until even and about 3 mm (⅛ inch) thick to make a crunchy pastry crust. See basic pastry on page 30 for guidance. Chill in the fridge for about 30 minutes while you make the frangipane.

Preheat the oven to 170°C / 325°F / Gas Mark 3. Mix the milled flax seeds with the water and leave for about 15 minutes to form a gel. Stir occasionally. Lightly toast the hazelnuts in the oven for 5–7 minutes on the prepared tray. When cool, remove the skins and blitz the nuts in a food processor – some should be finely ground while the rest are in slightly larger pieces. Combine the blitzed hazelnuts with the ground hazelnuts, cacao and salt, add the chocolate and then mix in the melted coconut oil, honey and hazelnut butter. Finally fold in the flax seed mix.

Line the tart tin with the pastry (see page 31). The pastry will break apart so gently push it together to make sure all the gaps are filled. Chill again in the fridge while you peel and core the pears and cut them into eighths.

Once chilled, smooth out any gaps in the pastry and push it up the edges, slightly overlapping the top of the shell, then trim off the edges. Place a piece of baking parchment in the pastry case and blind bake (see page 31) for 5 minutes, remove the baking beans, rotate the tray and bake for a further 5 minutes.

Remove from the oven, cool for 5 minutes and then fill with the frangipane, spreading it evenly. Arrange the pear slices on top. Bake for 10 minutes, rotate the tray and bake for a further 10–15 minutes. Leave to cool in the tin for about 20 minutes, glaze with apricot jam (jelly), and then remove. Serve warm from the oven with vanilla cashew 'yogurt' (see page 53) or dairy-free ice cream. This is best eaten fresh but will keep in an airtight container for up to three days.

### NOTE
*I love raw honey in the frangipane, but if you do not eat honey, try replacing it with your preferred liquid sweetener, such as maple syrup or coconut nectar.*

# Gooseberry and almond tart

........................................................................................

*I adore gooseberries! During the summer, I'll often go outside and graze on them in the garden after supper, when they've become a little softer and extra plump. Their tart flavour is perfectly balanced by the creamy sweet almond frangipane in this tart, while my 'basic pastry' used for the shell proves its versatility once more.*

........................................................................................

*Serves 10–12*

½ x recipe basic pastry (see page 30), rolled to 3 mm (⅛ inch) thick

**Frangipane**
125 g (4½ oz / ¾ cup plus 1½ tbsp) whole almonds, preferably activated dried (see page 25)
110 g (4 oz / ½ cup) non-hydrogenated dairy-free butter
80 g (2¾ oz / scant ⅔ cup) coconut sugar
½ tsp coarse sea salt, ground
Finely grated zest of ½ lemon
2 eggs plus 1 extra yolk
50 g (1¾ oz / scant ½ cup) ground almonds (almond meal)

**Topping**
300 g (10½ oz / 2 cups) gooseberries, fresh or frozen, tops and stems removed
Coconut sugar, to sprinkle
50 g (1¾ oz / generous ½ cup) flaked almonds
3 tbsp raw honey, optional

Preheat the oven to 170°C / 325°F / Gas Mark 3. Line a 23 cm (9 inch) loose-bottomed tart tin with pastry and blind bake (see page 31) for 10–15 minutes, until the edges are golden brown. Remove the baking beans and bake for a further 10 minutes, until light brown but not fully cooked.

For the frangipane filling, toast the almonds for 6–8 minutes on a baking tray lined with baking parchment, until just colouring, then leave to cool. By hand or using a freestanding mixer fitted with a paddle, cream the butter and coconut sugar with the salt and lemon zest until smooth and creamy. Add the eggs, one by one, but not the extra yolk. In a food processor, process the toasted almonds but do not grind them fully, we still want some texture. Finally add the chopped toasted almonds and ground almonds (almond meal) to the butter and egg mix and combine well until smooth. Do not worry if the mix looks a little split, it will still bake well.

Let the pastry base cool slightly and then brush the yolk over the pastry and bake for 2 more minutes. This forms a seal between the pastry and filling to keep it crunchy and stop it from getting soggy. Remove from the oven and cool for about 10 minutes.

Fill with the frangipane, top with the gooseberries, pressed into the frangipane, a sprinkling of coconut sugar and the flaked almonds. Bake for about 30 minutes, rotating the tart halfway through baking, until the top and almonds are golden and the gooseberries around the edge are just starting to brown. Leave to cool, demould onto a serving plate and drizzle the top of the tart with raw honey or serve it alongside the tart, if you want.

Serve warm as it is or cold with whipped vanilla coconut cream (see page 27), natural yogurt or ice cream. This is best eaten fresh but should keep well for up to three days in the fridge.

### NOTES
*For a vegan almond frangipane, make the frangipane used in the Raspberry and rose tartlets with pistachio frangipane (see page 118) but replace the pistachio nuts with almonds, the pistachio paste with almond butter and double the recipe for this 23 cm (9 inch) tart.*

*This tart works well with frozen gooseberries, so it can be enjoyed at any time of the year, or try it with other ripe seasonal fruits such as pears, raspberries or apricots.*

# Roasted root vegetable tarts with spiced sesame crust

*These sublime savoury tarts pack a super flavour punch. A spicy base made with sesame seeds and toasted pecans is covered in a light and creamy cashew béchamel, all topped off with an abundant mix of sweet and earthy carrots and beetroot. They are grain-free, vegan and perfect for a comforting but light lunch or supper.*

*Makes 6 tarts*

### Roasted root vegetables

4 large carrots, about 600 g (1 lb 5 oz)

4 beetroot, about 550 g (1 lb 3 oz)

2 onions

2 large cloves garlic, finely chopped or crushed

3 tbsp EVCP rapeseed oil or coconut oil, melted, plus extra for greasing

Coarse sea salt

Black pepper, optional

Generous bunch of fresh herbs such as coriander (cilantro) and parsley, finely chopped

### Spiced sesame and pecan crust

170 g (6 oz / 1½ cups) ground pecan nuts

105 g (3¾ oz / scant 1 cup) ground almonds (almond meal)

½ tsp each ground coriander, cumin, turmeric, ginger and cardamom

1½ tsp coarse sea salt

65 ml (2¼ fl oz / ¼ cup) EVCP rapeseed oil

2 tbsp filtered water

85 g (3 oz / ⅔ cup) black and white sesame seeds

### Cashew béchamel

25 g (¾ oz / 2 tbsp) coconut oil

40 g (1½ oz / generous ⅓ cup) gram flour

1 tsp Dijon mustard

450 ml (15 fl oz / scant 2 cups) cashew milk (see page 28)

3 tsp nutritional yeast flakes

Coarse sea salt and black pepper to taste

Preheat the oven to 175°C / 345°F / Gas Mark 3½. Grease six round 10 x 2 cm deep (4 x ¾ inch) tartlet tins.

Peel and cut the tops off the carrots. Cut them lengthways into about 3 cm (1¼ inch) long pieces, then quarter into small crudité-sized strips. Scrub the beetroot, quarter them and slice the same thickness as the carrots. Peel, quarter and slice the onions. On a large baking tray, mix up the vegetables with the garlic, oil and a generous amount of salt and black pepper, if using. Roast for about 1 hour, checking halfway through. They are ready when a skewer inserts easily into the centre of the vegetables. Remove from the oven, adjust the seasoning while still warm, and set aside.

Meanwhile, to make the base, combine the ground pecans, almonds, spices, salt, oil and water in a food processor. Add the sesame seeds and blitz until the mix looks like breadcrumbs and sticks together when you pick up a piece of it in your hand. Divide the pastry mix between the greased tins, you will get about 70 g (2½ oz) per tart, and press it down with your fingertips and a step palette knife (frosting spatula) to make the crust, pressing it into the edges and making sure it is even. Put the tins on a baking tray and bake in the same oven as the vegetables for about 15–20 minutes or until dark golden brown. Leave to cool.

To make the béchamel, melt the coconut oil in a small saucepan. Add the gram flour and whisk in vigorously. Add the mustard and then gradually start to add the cashew milk, stirring constantly with a whisk. The sauce should start to thicken and look smooth. Add the yeast flakes and salt and pepper to taste. Stir again and taste and season more if necessary. You can make this in advance for use later, but note that when it cools it will thicken slightly, so before filling your tarts with it, return to the heat and add some extra milk to loosen.

Finish off the vegetables by adding the freshly chopped herbs and a drizzle of extra virgin olive oil, if necessary. Mix the béchamel with a whisk until really smooth, use it to fill the tarts and then top with all of the vegetables, pushing them into the béchamel slightly. Serve with salad or steamed green vegetables.

These tarts are great served warm or cold and keep well for three days in the fridge.

### NOTE
*To make one large tart, line a 27–28 cm (10½–11 inch) tart tin with the above quantity of pastry and increase the baking time to 15–20 minutes or until dark golden brown, then fill as above.*

# Tomato and pepper pissaladière

Serves 4 as a main course or 6–8 as
a light starter

**Tomato and pepper filling**

1 red pepper
1 yellow pepper
1 orange pepper
2 tbsp EVCP rapeseed oil
2 onions, finely chopped
1 large garlic clove, crushed or finely
  chopped
1 x 400 g (14 oz) can chopped tomatoes
Small pinch crushed dried chillies, or
  more if you want!
Generous pinch of coarse sea salt
Black pepper
¼ tsp coconut sugar, optional
1 tbsp chopped oregano, plus extra for
  garnish
1 tbsp thyme leaves, plus extra for
  garnish
1 small handful basil or purple basil,
  plus extra for garnish
Anchovies, optional
12–15 black olives, Greek style

**Hazelnut pastry**

45 g (1½ oz/⅓ cup) whole hazelnuts,
  preferably activated dried (see
  page 25)
95 g (3¼ oz/⅔ cup) buckwheat flour
45 g (1½ oz/⅓ cup plus 1 tbsp) ground
  hazelnuts or ground almonds (almond
  meal)
12.5 g (scant ½ oz/1½ tbsp) arrowroot
1 tsp coarse sea salt, finely ground
50 g (1¾ oz/¼ cup) coconut oil
4 tbsp cold filtered water

*Perfect picnic food, this is my light and summery vegetarian take on the classic
Provençal savoury tart, which is made with caramelized onions, black olives and
anchovies. I have added tomatoes and herbs to the onions, while slithers of sweet
colourful peppers replace the anchovies, but you can include anchovies if you wish.
This is dedicated to an old family friend, Robert.*

Start by making the filling. Preheat the oven to 200°C/400°F/Gas Mark 6. Line a
baking tray with baking parchment.

Place the peppers on the lined baking tray and bake on the top shelf of the oven.
The skins will blister and char slightly, so turn them about every 5 minutes so
that the skins are blistered all over. You can also char them under a preheated
grill (broiler) if you wish.

Take out of the oven, remove from the baking tray and carefully cover with
cling film (plastic wrap). The moisture from the condensation will make the
skins easy to peel off. When completely cool, peel the peppers, using a small
knife if necessary, and rinse under running water to get rid of any bits of skin
and the seeds. Then slice into strips.

In a saucepan, heat the rapeseed oil. Add the onions and garlic, reduce the heat
and cook until soft, about 10 minutes. Add the tomatoes and continue cooking on
a low heat for a further 5 minutes. Add the chilli, seasoning to taste and sugar, if
using (I find it helps bring out the sweet tomato flavour), and continue to cook
for about 5 more minutes, until the sauce is thick, sweet, well seasoned and most
of the tomato juices have been cooked out. If too runny, the pastry will get soggy.
Remove from the heat and set aside to cool. Add the chopped herbs when cool.

Turn down the oven to 170°C/325°F/Gas Mark 3. Grease a 22 cm (8¾ inch)
ceramic pastry dish with coconut oil. Line a small baking tray with baking
parchment.

Spread out the whole hazelnuts on the baking tray and toast for 5 minutes. Leave
to cool then remove the skins and chop in a food processor until very fine, but
still with some texture. Mix the flour with all the ground nuts, the arrowroot and
salt. Melt the coconut oil and combine it with the dry ingredients, followed by the
water. Mix to combine, adding a little more water if necessary to stick, and bring
the mix together into a rough ball.

Line the pastry dish with the pastry and blind bake (see pages 30–31) for 10
minutes. Remove from the oven, take out the baking beans, rotate and bake for a
further 10 minutes, or until a rich golden brown. Leave to cool then fill with the
tomato mix. Arrange the pepper slices and anchovies, if using, over the tomato
mix, followed by the olives and then finish with the oregano, thyme leaves and
basil sprigs. Drizzle with a little extra virgin olive oil, if you want.

This is best eaten fresh but will keep for up to three days in the fridge.

# Quince pies

*Makes 24 quince pies with leftover
baked quince mincemeat*

600 g (1lb 5 oz) quince (2–3 quince)

1 tbsp coconut oil, melted

1 x recipe basic pastry (see page 30),
rolled out to about 3 mm (⅛ inch)
thick

50 g (1¾ oz/⅓ cup) unsulphured dried
apricots

100 g (3½ oz/⅔ cup) dates

100 g (3½ oz/scant ⅔ cup) raisins

100 g (3½ oz/⅔ cup) currants

100 g (3½ oz/⅔ cup) sultanas (seedless
golden raisins)

25 g (¾ oz/3 tbsp) almonds, preferably
soaked for 8–12 hours or activated
dried (see page 25), roughly chopped

15 g (½ oz/2½ tbsp) peeled ginger,
finely chopped

¼ whole nutmeg, grated

½ tsp mixed spice

¼ tsp ground cloves

¼ tsp ground cinnamon

Finely grated zest and juice of ½
large orange

Finely grated zest and juice of ½
large lemon

50 g (1¾ oz/scant ¼ cup) easy apple
purée (see page 32)

¼ tsp coarse sea salt

1 tbsp raw honey or maple syrup

50 g (1¾ oz/¼ cup) coconut butter

*Christmas would not be the same without mince pies, bursting with rich dried fruits, spices and citrus notes. After a glut of quince one year, I decided to add them to the mix, rather than the usual grated apple, and this was the delicious result, giving the mix a sweet, tart twist. Freshly chopped ginger lifts all the flavours up.*

Preheat the oven to 160°C/310°F/Gas Mark 2½ and you will need two tartlet tins. Peel, core and cut the quince into eighths; you should have about 400 g (14 oz) of quince flesh. Place on a baking tray, drizzle with the melted coconut oil and bake for 30–40 minutes, or until tender. Turn up the oven to 170°C/325°F/Gas Mark 3.

Cut out 24 rounds of pastry with a cookie cutter, large enough to fit your tartlet holes, and press the pastry in gently. I like to use a 6 cm (2½ inch) fluted cutter, but a plain one is fine. Cut out 24 tops (either make traditional plain round tops or cut out shapes like stars, hearts or holly) and place on a tray lined with baking parchment. Chill the tart cases and tops in the fridge until needed.

In a food processor, blitz the apricots and dates until small pieces. Add half the raisins, currants and sultanas (seedless golden raisins) and blitz again. You want the mix to all come together and be in small pieces, almost like mince, but not a paste. When the quince has cooled, add it to the dried fruits and blitz again until almost pulp but with some texture.

Remove from the food processor, tip into a large bowl and add the rest of the raisins, currants and sultanas (seedless golden raisins), the chopped almonds, ginger, spices, orange and lemon zest and juice, apple purée, salt and honey or maple syrup. Grate in the coconut butter, or finely chop it. Mix everything together with your hands, squeezing the mix through your fingers to make sure it is all really well combined and there are no large lumps of coconut butter.

Fill the lined tartlets with a generous amount of the quince mincemeat and then top with your prepared pastry discs or shapes. If you are using discs, slice a small cross in the middle of each pie disc using a sharp knife. Bake for 10–12 minutes, rotating the tray halfway, until the tops are golden-brown. Serve straight from the oven or leave to cool and then warm up when needed.

These quince pies last for at least five days in an airtight container. The mincemeat will keep for up to ten days in a sealed glass jar in the fridge or you can freeze it. It's best to make this quince mincemeat fresh every year – I do this by storing quinces from October.

### NOTES

*I have given the amount of pastry to make 24 quince pies, but the quincemeat is enough to make at least 40 quince pies so increase or decrease the quantities accordingly if you prefer. I like to make one big batch fresh every year, bake off about half, and then keep the rest in the fridge or freezer ready for impromptu visits from family and friends, of which there seem to be a lot at Christmas!*

*Freeze any leftover pastry for at least one month or bake off as biscuits (cookies).*

# Maple baked apple pies

............................................................................................

**Makes 12 small pies**

Coconut oil, for greasing
1 x recipe basic pastry (see page 30),
    rolled out to 3 mm (⅛ inch) thick
400 g (14 oz) peeled and cored dessert
    apples such as Egremont Russet or
    Cox
Finely grated zest of ½ lemon
40 ml (1½ fl oz/8 tsp) lemon juice
Pinch Himalayan pink salt
1 tsp ground cinnamon
460 g (1 lb/scant 2 cups) easy apple
    purée (see page 32)
120 g (4¼ oz/⅓ cup plus 1 tbsp) maple
    syrup

*Apple, maple syrup and cinnamon is a classic heavenly marriage of flavours. I urge you to find the best-quality, local apples; without them, these pies will be insipidly sad. I adore Egremont Russets with their crisp sweetness and rich unique flavour, but Cox and other dessert apples also work well.*

............................................................................................

Preheat the oven to 170°C/325°F/Gas Mark 3 and grease a 12-hole muffin tin with coconut oil (or your preferred dairy-free oil or butter).

Using a round 10 cm (4 inch) cookie cutter, cut out 12 discs of pastry and carefully push one into each mould. The pastry will break apart, so carefully push it back together with your fingertips, smoothing it out so there are no gaps. If the pastry comes up around the edges of the moulds, trim it off with a small sharp knife. Cut out 12 tops using a cutter no larger than 9 cm (3½ inch). Once lined, put the muffin tray and the pastry tops in the fridge to chill. Any leftover pastry can be frozen for at least 1 month.

Cut the apple into cubes, each about ½ cm (⅕ inch). Combine the cubed apple, lemon zest and juice, salt, cinnamon and apple purée and mix well. Add the maple syrup, use less if you want to your taste, and stir to combine. Divide the mix between the 12 lined shells, you should get about 80 g (2¾ oz) of mix per pie. Finish off each pie with the cut-out pastry top, pressing it down to stick to the shell. Cut a small cross in the top of each pie and bake for about 15 minutes, rotating the tray halfway, until the tops are golden brown and slightly cracking on top. Leave to cool in the tins.

To demould, use a kitchen knife or small palette knife (frosting spatula) and slide it around the edge of each pie and then carefully lift them up from the bottom. The pies are likely to crumble if they are demoulded straight from the oven so make sure they have cooled slightly. Eat cold or warm with vanilla ice cream or whipped coconut cream (see page 27), heating the pies up for about 5 minutes in a medium oven if wanted warm. Dust with a little agave sugar if you wish.

These are best eaten fresh, but will keep well for about three days in a sealed container.

**NOTE**
*You can also make one large pie. Use the basic pastry recipe on page 30 and follow the method given for the Fig and raspberry pie on page 132, simply using the apple filling in this recipe.*

# Fig and raspberry pie with pistachio crème anglaise

*Serves 6–8*

### Chestnut crust

120 g (4¼ oz / 1 cup less 1½ tbsp) chestnut flour

120 g (4¼ oz / 1 cup plus 2 tbsp) ground almonds (almond meal)

45 g (1½ oz / ⅓ cup) coconut sugar

Finely grated zest of ½ lemon

½ tsp coarse sea salt, finely ground

1 egg plus 1 egg yolk, reserve the egg white

3 tsp cold filtered water

75 g (2¾ oz / ⅓ cup) coconut oil, plus extra for greasing

### Fig and raspberry filling

8 figs, about 350 g (12¼ oz), stalks removed and cut into sixths

250 g (8¾ oz / 2 cups) raspberries, fresh or frozen

30 g (1 oz / 1½ tbsp) raw honey

3 tsp lemon juice

¼ vanilla pod (bean), split lengthways and seeds scraped out, pod reserved

### Glaze

1 egg yolk

1 tbsp almond milk (see page 28)

Pinch Himalayan pink salt

### Pistachio crème anglaise

2 egg yolks

1½ tsp cornflour (cornstarch)

350 ml (12 fl oz / 1½ cups) pistachio milk (see page 28) (shell the soaked pistachio nuts before making your milk to make an extra pretty green crème anglaise)

½ vanilla pod (bean), split lengthways and seeds scraped out

55 g (2 oz / scant 3 tbsp) raw honey

*This grain-free pastry is perfectly sweet, mainly thanks to the wonderfully flavoursome chestnut flour and ground almonds (almond meal). When it's baked, it becomes a marzipan-like crust, encompassing meltingly tender honeyed figs and juicy raspberries, a true celebration of fresh seasonal produce at its best.*

Grease a pie dish about 21 x 15 x 5 cm deep (8¼ x 6 x 2 inch) with a 2 cm (¾ inch) rim (any pie dish with similar dimensions will work) with coconut oil and preheat the oven to 170°C / 325°F / Gas Mark 3. Make the crust by hand or in a freestanding mixer. With a paddle, combine the chestnut flour, ground almonds (almond meal), coconut sugar, lemon zest and salt. In a separate bowl, mix together the egg, extra yolk and cold water. Melt the coconut oil and add to the dry ingredients while stirring, followed by the egg and water mix. Stir until everything is completely combined. It will be quite sticky, but that's normal.

Bring the crust mix together in your hands and weigh out 250 g (8¾ oz). Roll it out between two pieces of floured baking parchment until it is about 3 mm (⅛ inch) thick (see basic pastry on page 30). Take off the top layer of parchment and flip the pastry into the pie dish. It will collapse a little, but do not worry. Piece it back together, making sure there are no holes. The pastry will be soft so work quickly. Trim off the edges, leaving a little pastry coming up over the edges. Bake the base for 10 minutes or until golden brown. The edges will be slightly darker, but that's fine. Leave to cool a little. Brush with the reserved egg white and bake for 5 minutes or until dried out. Roll out the rest of the pastry using the same method as before and refrigerate.

In a large bowl, mix the filling ingredients together and pour into the baked shell. Top with the remaining refrigerated pastry, trimming the edges if necessary, and then crimp them using your thumb and index finger. Whisk together the glaze ingredients and glaze the pie. Make a cross in the centre of the pie and bake for 15–20 minutes until the top is golden brown and the edges slightly darker.

Meanwhile, make the pistachio crème anglaise. Using a whisk, combine the egg yolks with the cornflour (cornstarch) in a large bowl. In a saucepan, heat the pistachio milk, vanilla seeds, empty pod (bean) and honey and when it is just about to boil, gradually pour the milk over the egg yolks, while whisking. Pour everything back into the saucepan and stir on a low–medium heat using a whisk. If the heat is too high, your yolks will scramble. Keep mixing until the anglaise reaches 82°C / 180°F. If you do not have a thermometer, the mix is ready when it is thick enough to coat the back of a spoon and leave a trail if you run your finger through the coating. Pour through a fine sieve and transfer into a jug. It does not need to be served hot so keep it on one side and mix with a spoon before serving. Taste and adjust sweetness if desired. Serve with the pie, warm from the oven. The pie and crème anglaise are best eaten on the day they are made.

### NOTE
*I also make this just with raspberries, and it's totally sublime. Thankfully this pie is so versatile, any sweet seasonal fruits will work – plums, blackberries, apples and pears all make fitting substitutions – just make sure your pie is jam-packed with fruit!*

# Baked kabocha squash pie

*Serves 8–10*

**Kabocha squash purée**
*Makes 750 g (1 lb 10 oz/3⅓ cups) squash purée*
1.1 kg (2 lb 7 oz) whole kabocha squash (weight of flesh about 850 g (1 lb 14 oz))
1 tbsp coconut oil, melted
150 ml (5 fl oz/scant ⅔ cup) water

**Kabocha squash pie**
Coconut oil, for greasing
320 g (11 oz) basic pastry (see page 30), rolled to 3 mm (⅛ inch) thick
1 egg yolk
90 g (3 oz/¾ cup) coconut sugar
¼ tsp Himalayan pink salt
1 tsp ground cinnamon
½ tsp ground ginger
½ tsp ground cloves
Generous grating of nutmeg
450 g (1 lb/2 cups) kabocha squash purée (see above)
225 ml (7½ fl oz/scant 1 cup) cashew milk (see page 28)
75 g (2¾ oz/scant ⅓ cup) easy apple purée (see page 32)
2 eggs

*Like a pumpkin pie, but better! This is richer and more full of flavour thanks to the luxuriously creamy purée, which creates the base of the warming spiced filling.*
*I have chosen kabocha squash instead of pumpkin, as I love its rich chestnut flavour and the creamy thick purée it creates, not to mention its bright and vibrant colour.*

Preheat the oven to 170°C/325°F/Gas Mark 3.

Peel, de-seed and chop the squash into rough 2.5 cm (1 inch) cubes. Place on a baking tray, drizzle with the coconut oil and roast for about 20–30 minutes until soft and a skewer inserts easily into the centre of a piece. Leave to cool – the cooked weight will be about 620 g (1 lb 6 oz).

Blend the squash with the water until really smooth. Do persevere if it's taking a while to get smooth as the lovely thick purée really makes this pie. If you think you need more water, add as little as possible. Use immediately or freeze for use in the future.

Grease a 22 x 4 cm deep (8¾ x 1½ inch) pie dish with coconut oil. Line the dish with the rolled pastry (see page 31). Chill for about 20 minutes in the fridge then blind bake (see page 31) for 15 minutes. Remove the baking beans and bake for a further 10–15 minutes, until the pastry is golden brown. Brush the pastry with the egg yolk and cook for a further 3 minutes until the yolk is dry. This will seal the pastry and ensure that it won't go soggy when the mix is added. Reduce the oven to 160°C/310°F/Gas Mark 2½.

Combine the pie ingredients together in a large bowl and blend with a hand-held blender until completely smooth. The mix will look quite thick, but this is normal. Pour the mix into the baked tart tin and bake for 20 minutes. Rotate the pie and reduce the heat to 150°C/300°F/Gas Mark 2 and bake for a further 10–20 minutes. The pie is ready when it has formed a slight skin on top and when you lightly shake it, it should feel set and firm but with a very slight wobble.

Leave to cool completely before serving. Serve with whipped vanilla coconut cream (see page 27). This is best eaten fresh but keeps in the fridge for about three days.

**NOTE**
*For this pie it really pays to make your own purée. Any leftover purée can be frozen.*

Raw desserts

# Mango, coconut and lime chia puddings with mint

*Serves 4 for pudding or 2 for breakfast*

4 tbsp chia seeds
2 tbsp milled flax seeds
180 ml (6 fl oz / ¾ cup) coconut milk,
  plus extra to drizzle, optional
50 ml (1¾ fl oz / scant ¼ cup) juice from
  1–2 limes
250 g (8¾ oz) mango flesh (about 1
  mango), plus extra for serving
10 medium–large mint leaves
Pinch Himalayan pink salt
Generous pinch ground cardamom
1 tsp baobab powder, optional
50 g (1¾ oz) ice cubes

### Toppings

Natural coconut yogurt, optional
Bee pollen, optional
Goji berries, optional, soaked for 10
  minutes in warm water to soften
Fresh mint leaves, optional
Fresh or dried coconut, optional

*Packed with protein and omega 3 fatty acids, chia seeds are a great start to the day, although their texture is an acquired taste! So here, I whizz them up in a blender with mango, mint and coconut milk to make a delectably smooth and creamy pudding that's fresh and fragrant at the same time. It's a real winner!*

Combine the chia seeds and milled flax seeds with the coconut milk. Stir well and leave for at least 15 minutes to swell up, or make the night before, as I do, and leave to swell up in the fridge until the next day.

Put the soaked seeds in a blender with the rest of the ingredients, and baobab powder if using, leaving the ice cubes until last. Blend until completely smooth, then add the ice cubes for extra freshness. Blend once more until completely smooth. Pour out into the glasses and layer with cubes of fresh mango if desired. Finish with your preferred toppings, drizzle with a little extra coconut milk, if you wish, and serve immediately.

This will keep well in the fridge for at least three days, so make a large batch at the beginning of the week. Enjoy it on its own for breakfast, or add extras like homemade granola, seeds, nuts and fresh fruit.

### VARIATION

*Creamy avocado and lime chia pudding*
To half the avocado lime cream filling in the Courgette (zucchini), basil, lime and pistachio cake on page 36, mix in 6 tbsp of chia seeds and leave to swell for at least 15 minutes at room temperature or overnight in the fridge. Stir in coconut milk to loosen if necessary before serving. Serves as a delectably creamy pudding or breakfast.

### NOTES

*You can use other fruits in place of the mango, such as papaya or kiwi fruit, berries or ripe stoned fruits when in season.*

*Baobab powder is made from the ground seeds of the baobab fruit. Its strong citrus notes of orange and grapefruit hint at its nutrient-dense profile – high in fibre and rich in vitamin C, calcium, potassium and thiamin. It also has one of the highest antioxidant capacities of any fruit in the world. I love to add it to raw desserts, as above, as well as to smoothies.*

*Antioxidant-rich, goji berries have a strong sweetness and slight sharpness. I love them plumped up in my Super-berry cashew 'yogurt' on page 72, and they're great sprinkled on breakfasts or added to salads, cakes, muffins and raw chocolate. For similar use, I like Incan berries, also known as golden or Aztec berries, with impressive nutrients including many B vitamins, vitamin A and C; and white mulberries, containing iron, calcium, fibre and anthocyanins. Incan berries are the most sour of the three berries, but sweet at the same time, while mulberries are very sweet with a grape-like flavour. Try them in your cooking and in my Wonder berry chocolate bars on page 156.*

# Tiramisù mousse

*'Coconut milk, coconut oil and avocado, all in a tiramisù, excuse me?' I hear you say. But do not fear! These amazingly versatile dairy-free substitutes create velvety, light, well-flavoured layers of sublime mousse. Everything just melts together to create a cloud-like light and creamy coffee and vanilla 'pick-me-up' pudding.*

*Serves 4*

**Vanilla cream**

2 x 400 ml (14 fl oz) cans of coconut milk
50 g (1¾ oz / 2½ tbsp) blonde coconut
  nectar or raw clear honey
½ vanilla pod (bean), split lengthways
  and seeds scraped out

**Coffee mousse**

25 g (¾ oz / 5 tbsp) ground coffee
150 ml (5 fl oz / scant ⅔ cup) boiling
  water
150 ml (5 fl oz / scant ⅔ cup) coconut
  milk
150 g (5¼ oz) avocado (about 1 large
  avocado)
70 g (2½ oz / scant ¼ cup)
  maple syrup
1 tsp cacao powder
1 tsp carob powder
Pinch Himalayan pink salt
1 tsp vanilla extract
20 g (¾ oz / 1½ tbsp) coconut oil

**To decorate**

A few cubes homemade chocolate
  (see page 156) or dark (bittersweet)
  chocolate 85% cocoa solids

The night before, put the two cans of coconut milk in the fridge for the vanilla cream. You will also need four tall but wide glasses, coupes or bowls.

Open the refrigerated cans of coconut milk and scrape off the thicker part of the milk. You need 450 g (1 lb / scant 2 cups) thick set milk for the vanilla cream. Set aside in the fridge until needed. Reserve the rest of the coconut milk for the coffee mousse.

To make the coffee mousse, combine the ground coffee and boiling water and set aside. Place 150 ml (5 fl oz / scant ⅔ cup) of coconut milk into a blender. Place the rest of the mousse ingredients, except the coffee and coconut oil, in the blender and blend until smooth. Melt the coconut oil and add to the blender. Strain the coffee, measure out 60 ml (2 fl oz / ¼ cup) and add to the blender, blending until completely smooth. Spoon out 55 g (2 oz) of the coffee mousse into each glass and refrigerate.

Next make the vanilla cream. Take the set coconut milk and whip until smooth and thick using a hand-held whisk or freestanding mixer, then add the coconut nectar or honey and vanilla and whisk once more. Remove the glasses from the fridge and spoon 40 g (1½ oz) of vanilla cream over each layer of coffee mousse. Divide the rest of the coffee mousse over the first layer of vanilla cream, then top with a final layer of cream according to the size of your glasses. Be careful as you layer it as the layers will be soft. Refrigerate until needed, grate chocolate over the top, serve with any leftover cream and enjoy.

# Velvet chocolate pots

*While many chocolate desserts can be heavy and cloying, coconut yogurt adds a subtle surprising freshness to these pots, but the flavour of coconut is not detectable, nor is the avocado's. Instead, they combine to create a seductively smooth mousse-like cream, which is rich but light at the same time and beats all its rivals!*

*Serves 6*

160 g (5½ oz) avocado (about 1 large
  avocado)
200 g (7 oz / ¾ cup plus 1 tbsp) chocolate
  coconut yogurt
100 g (3½ oz / ¼ cup plus ½ tbsp)
  date syrup
15 g (½ oz / 3 tbsp) cacao powder, plus
  extra to dust
½ tsp vanilla extract
Pinch Himalayan pink salt
60 g (2 oz / generous ¼ cup) coconut oil

You will need 6 small ramekins, teacups or small suitable pots. Place everything except the coconut oil in the blender and process. Melt the coconut oil, add to the chocolate mix and blend on full speed until completely smooth. Divide the mix evenly between the cups and place in the fridge for an hour to chill slightly and set. Remove from the fridge, dust with cacao powder and serve immediately. If you refrigerate the pots for longer than this then remove them from the fridge about an hour before serving. They will keep for up to three days in the fridge, depending on the freshness of the avocado and yogurt.

**Overleaf:** *Velvet chocolate pots and Chocolate truffle teff brownies (see page 103).*

# Summer fruit tart

*Serves 10–14*

**Raw tart base**

180 g (6¼ oz) figs

140 g (5 oz / 1 cup) almonds, preferably activated dried (see page 25)

140 g (5 oz / generous 1 cup) cashew nuts, preferably activated dried (see page 25)

½ vanilla pod (bean), cut lengthways and seeds scraped out

½ tsp Himalayan pink salt

Finely grated zest of ½ orange

40 ml (8 tsp) orange juice

70 g (2½ oz / ⅔ cup) ground almonds (almond meal)

1 x recipe quick-blend raw raspberry chia jam (jelly) (see page 32)

**Vanilla cream**

1 x recipe cashew cream (see page 27)

1 vanilla pod (bean), cut lengthways and seeds scraped out

40 g (1½ oz / scant 3 tbsp) blonde coconut nectar

2 tsp lemon juice

40 g (1½ oz / 3 tbsp) coconut oil, plus extra for greasing

About 1 kg (2 lbs 3 oz) fresh summer fruits (see note)

*Sometimes it is the simplest desserts that are the most delicious, and you cannot get more classic than fresh and juicy summer fruits with vanilla cream. Add a gorgeous raw tart base, raspberry chia jam (jelly) for a sweet tangy kick, then cut a slice, sit back, relax in the sun and enjoy.*

Lightly grease a loose-bottomed 28 cm (11 inch) tart tin with coconut oil. Soak the figs in filtered water for 30 minutes. Drain and remove the tops and roughly chop. In a food processor, roughly chop the nuts, keeping some large pieces. Remove from the food processor.

Place the soaked figs, vanilla seeds, salt, orange zest and juice in the food processor and blend to form a paste. Add the ground almonds (almond meal) and the chopped nuts and process until combined. Turn out the raw dough into the tin and press it down to make an even 'pastry' base. Cover with the raspberry chia jam (jelly) and refrigerate.

To make the vanilla cream, put the cashew cream, vanilla seeds, coconut nectar and lemon juice in a blender. Blend until smooth. Melt the coconut oil, add to the cream, and blend once more until completely smooth.

Remove the tart base from the fridge and cover the jam (jelly) layer with the vanilla cream. Return to the fridge for 3–4 hours to firm up slightly. Decorate with the fruit. Serve fresh when all the flavours and colours are at their best. Keep covered in the fridge for about three days.

**NOTE**

*All summer fruits work well here – try a mix of raspberries, strawberries, blueberries, apricots, peaches, nectarines, redcurrants, blackcurrants and white currants.*

# Strawberry verbena granita

*Serves 10*

150 ml (5 fl oz / scant ⅔ cup) filtered water

100 g (3½ oz / ¼ cup plus 1 tbsp) raw honey

3 tbsp dried lemon verbena

1 x 450 g (1 lb) cucumber, peeled and deseeded

300 g (10½ oz) strawberries

150 ml (5 fl oz / scant ⅔ cup) lime juice (from about 5 limes)

¼ tsp Himalayan pink salt

*When summer is at its peak, granitas are the best way to cool off. This one is cleansing, light, soft and delicately scented, perfect on a sunny day when you need a quick refreshing boost.*

In a small saucepan, bring the water, honey and lemon verbena just to a boil. Take off the heat and leave to infuse for 10 minutes. Put the cucumber, strawberries, lime juice and salt in a blender and blend until smooth. Add the sweet lemon verbena water, along with the leaves, and blend until completely smooth.

Pour into a freezer-proof container and freeze for about 2 hours or until the top has frozen. Remove from the freezer and scrape the frozen part with a fork, breaking it up into ice crystals. Repeat this process about 3 times, every 1–2 hours, until you get a texture of crushed, slightly slushy, ice. Then continue to freeze until needed. Serve in glasses.

## Chocolate 'biscuit' base

Coconut oil, for greasing

120 g (4¼ oz/¾ cup) pitted Medjool
   dates

25 g (¾ oz/3 tbsp) cashew nuts,
   preferably activated dried (see
   page 25)

1½ tsp vanilla extract

1¼ tbsp cacao powder

¼ tsp Himalayan pink salt

120 g (4¼ oz/scant ½ cup) almond
   butter (see page 26) or other nut butter

125 g (4½ oz/¾ cup) buckwheat groats,
   preferably activated dried (see
   page 25)

20 g (¾ oz) homemade chocolate (see
   page 156), or dark (bittersweet)
   chocolate 85% cocoa solids

20 g (¾ oz/2 tbsp) cacao nibs

## Banana and passionfruit filling

70 g (2½ oz/½ cup) cashew nuts

60 g (2 oz/generous ⅓ cup) pitted
   Medjool dates

½ tsp Himalayan pink salt

430 g (15¼ oz) very ripe banana flesh
   (3–4 bananas)

½ tsp ground cinnamon

½ vanilla pod (bean), split lengthways
   and seeds scraped out

70 g (2½ oz/⅓ cup) coconut oil, melted

About 8 small passionfruit

25 ml (¾ fl oz/5 tsp) lime juice

## Sticky toffee sauce

150 g (5¼ oz/1 cup) pitted Medjool
   dates

200 ml (7 fl oz/¾ cup) warm water

1 tsp coarse sea salt

½ vanilla pod (bean), split lengthways
   and seeds scraped out

75 ml (2½ fl oz/⅓ cup) coconut milk

## Decoration

1 large banana, about 180 g (6¼ oz)

40–50 g (1½–1¾ oz) homemade
   chocolate (see page 156) or dark
   (bittersweet) chocolate shards 85%
   cocoa solids

20 g (¾ oz/2 tbsp) buckwheat groats,
   activated dried (see page 25)

20 g (¾ oz/2 tbsp) cacao nibs

2 passionfruit

# Chocolate, banana and passion-fruit pie with sticky toffee sauce

...................................................................................

*The combination of chocolate with banana will never go out of fashion. This pie's bitter sweetness is perfectly balanced with the sea salt in the toffee sauce and the sharp passionfruit. With the cacao, nuts, banana, dates and the rest of the nourishing ingredients, this is one seriously tasty energy-boosting pie.*

...................................................................................

Soak the cashew nuts for the banana and passionfruit filling for 3–4 hours in 200 ml (7 fl oz/¾ cup plus 1 tbsp) of filtered water with a scant ½ tsp of Himalayan pink salt, then drain and rinse.

Grease the bottom and sides of a loose-bottomed 22 cm (8¾ inch) fluted tart tin, about 3.5 cm (1⅓ inch) deep, with coconut oil.

In a food processor, blitz the dates and cashew nuts for the base until small pieces and just coming together in a ball. Add the vanilla, cacao powder, salt and almond butter and process once more for about a minute. Finally add the buckwheat groats and blitz a few times until the groats start to break up and if you squeeze pieces of the mix it will stick together. Put into the prepared tart tin and press down and around the fluted edge until even. Leave to chill in the freezer.

Melt the chocolate slowly using a bain-marie (see page 156). Using a pastry brush, spread the bottom of the chocolate 'biscuit' base with the melted chocolate and then sprinkle over the cacao nibs. Freeze again.

For the filling, place the soaked cashew nuts in a blender with the dates, salt, banana, cinnamon and vanilla seeds, and blend until smooth. Scrape down the mix and blend once more. Pour in the coconut oil and blend again until totally smooth. Take out two-thirds (400 g/14 oz) of the mix and pour onto the 'biscuit' base. Spread it out until smooth, tap the surface to remove any air bubbles and return to the freezer.

Cut the passionfruits in half, remove all the pips and pulp and press through a fine sieve to get 80 ml (2¾ fl oz/⅓ cup) juice. Add the lime juice and then pour all the juice into the remaining banana mix in the blender, blending until everything is well combined. Pour the passion fruit layer on top of the banana layer and freeze once more for 3 hours or overnight.

For the sauce, soak the dates in the warm water for 10 minutes. Blend the dates and liquid with the salt, vanilla and coconut milk until smooth. Refrigerate until needed and mix well before use.

Defrost the pie in a cool place for 3 hours or in the refrigerator for 12 hours before serving. When defrosted but still cool, remove from the tin and transfer to a serving plate. Before serving decorate with slices of banana and chocolate shards, slightly pushing them into the filling, finishing off by sprinkling on buckwheat groats, cacao nibs and passionfruit seeds. Or serve it as it is, pouring over some of the sauce with each portion. The pie and the sauce will last well in the fridge for about five days.

# Pristine Black Forest parfait

........................................................................................

*Fresh sweet black cherries and dried sour cherries combine to make this vibrant and seductive raw layer cake. It's not only power-packed with flavour and texture but goodness too from the cacao, Brazil nuts and sprouted oat base to the sensuous creamy layers made with cashew nuts and coconut oil.*

........................................................................................

*Serves 10*

**Chocolate cake**

60 g (2 oz / scant ⅓ cup) Brazil nuts
80 g (2¾ oz / ½ cup) pitted Medjool dates
¼ vanilla pod (bean), split lengthways
    and seeds scraped out
½ tsp Himalayan pink salt
1 tbsp cacao powder
½ tsp ground cinnamon
40 g (1½ oz) homemade chocolate,
    see page 156, or dark (bittersweet)
    chocolate 85% cocoa solids, roughly
    chopped
40 g (1½ oz / scant ⅓ cup) sprouted oats

**Vanilla layer**

100 g (3½ oz / ¾ cup) cashew nuts
70 ml (2½ fl oz / ¼ cup plus 2 tsp)
    almond milk (see page 28)
30 g (1 oz / 2 tbsp) blonde coconut nectar
    or raw clear honey
½ vanilla pod (bean), split lengthways
    and seeds scraped out
50 g (1¾ oz / ¼ cup) coconut oil, melted

**Cherry layer**

100 g (3½ oz / ¾ cup) cashew nuts
200 g (7 oz / 1½ cups) pitted fresh
    cherries
¼ tsp ground cinnamon
¼ tsp Himalayan pink salt
Finely grated zest of ¼ lemon
3 tsp lemon juice
100 g (3½ oz / ½ cup) coconut oil
50 g (1¾ oz / ⅓ cup) dried sour cherries
10–20 g (⅓–¾ oz / 2–4 tsp) coconut
    nectar or raw honey, optional

Soak the cashew nuts for each layer separately in 200 ml (7 fl oz / ¾ cup plus 1 tbsp) of filtered water with a scant ½ tsp of Himalayan pink salt for 3–4 hours. Drain and rinse well.

Line a baking tray at least 27 cm (10½ inches) long and 4 cm (1½ inches) deep with baking parchment.

In a food processor, roughly chop the Brazil nuts for the cake. Remove from the processor, then add the dates, vanilla seeds, salt, cacao powder and cinnamon to the blender and blitz to make a paste. Add the chopped nuts, chocolate and sprouted oats, and pulse a few times to combine. The mix will be in crumbs but should come together when you squeeze a piece in your hands.

Turn out the raw cake mix and press it along one long and one short edge of the baking tray to make a 26.5 x 9 cm (10½ x 3½ inch) rectangular base. Now you need to make a make-shift mould around the cake base. Fold up a piece of aluminium foil, overlapping it about three times to make a 4 cm (1½ inch) high wall. Place the wall around the two edges of the cake that aren't touching the baking tray. Freeze.

Make the vanilla layer. Blend the soaked cashew nuts and almond milk until smooth. Add the coconut nectar or honey, vanilla seeds and coconut oil and blend until completely smooth. Pour over the chocolate base, making sure none of the mix leaks through the mould. Freeze immediately to set (1–2 hours). The vanilla layer must be completely set before adding the cherry layer.

Make the cherry layer. Place the cherries, cinnamon, salt, lemon zest and juice in the blender and process to make a cherry juice. Add the soaked cashew nuts and blend until almost completely smooth. Melt the coconut oil and add it to the blender, along with the sour cherries, and blend once more until completely smooth, scraping the mix down from the sides if necessary. The mix should turn from a deep purple to red when the sour cherries are added. Taste and adjust to your preferred sweetness if desired. Pour the cherry layer over the vanilla layer and freeze for a further 1 hour until firm but not frozen solid. Remove from the freezer and slice into 2.5 cm (1 inch) wide rectangles. To get a clean cut, dip a sharp knife in hot water and slice when frozen.

Decorate each piece as you want to. I love to use cacao nibs, fresh cherries and edible flowers. If you are feeling particularly naughty, make a batch of the Chocolate silk glaze on page 151 to serve with it. Keeps in the fridge for five days. This can be frozen for up to three months but it needs to be defrosted before serving as it should be served like a cold mousse.

*NOTE*
*In season, red-pink cherries are a must for this, otherwise you won't achieve the right colour. You can also add a little beetroot powder if you are not satisfied with the colour.*

## Crystallized salted nuts

50 g (1¾ oz / ⅓ cup) pine nuts

50 g (1¾ oz / ⅓ cup) pistachios, preferably activated dried (see page 25)

20 g (¾ oz / 1 tbsp) maple syrup

20 g (¾ oz / 2 tbsp) coconut sugar

½ tsp Himalayan pink salt

## Walnut and pistachio base

100 g (3½ oz / ⅔ cup) dried figs

85 g (3 oz / ¾ cup) walnuts, preferably activated dried (see page 25)

85 g (3 oz / ⅔ cup) pistachios, preferably activated dried (see page 25)

½ vanilla pod (bean), cut lengthways and seeds scraped out

¼ tsp Himalayan pink salt

Finely grated zest of ¼ orange

30 g (1 oz / ¼ cup) ground almonds (almond meal)

## Bitter orange ice cream

150 g (5¼ oz / 1 cup plus 2 tbsp) macadamia nuts

175 g (6 oz / scant 1¼ cups) pitted Medjool dates

400 ml (14 fl oz / 1¾ cups) orange juice

180 ml (6 fl oz / ¾ cup) coconut milk

½ vanilla pod (bean), cut lengthways and seeds scraped out

Finely grated zest of 1 orange

¼ tsp Himalayan pink salt

1 tsp lemon juice

2 tsp orange extract

## Chocolate orange ice cream

2 tbsp cacao powder

45 g (1½ oz / ⅓ cup) pitted Medjool dates

½ tsp Himalayan pink salt

60 ml (2 fl oz / ¼ cup) coconut milk

50 g (1¾ oz) homemade chocolate (see page 156) or dark (bittersweet) chocolate 85% cocoa solids

## Chocolate silk glaze

80 g (2¾ oz / ⅓ cup) coconut oil, melted

160 g (5½ oz / ½ cup) maple syrup

70 g (2½ oz / scant ⅔ cup) cacao powder

½ vanilla pod (bean), split lengthways and seeds scraped out

Pinch Himalayan pink salt

50 ml (1¾ fl oz / ¼ cup) filtered water

# Bitter chocolate orange ice cream cake with chocolate glaze

*This fun but sophisticated stripy cake marries two flavours that were born to be together – chocolate and orange and their sensuous bittersweet notes. Thin layers of homemade chocolate crack between the ice cream while the intense flavours of the filling are rounded off with salty-sweet crunchy nuts.*

Soak the macadamia nuts for the bitter orange ice cream for 6 hours in 300 ml (10½ fl oz / 1¼ cups) of filtered water with ½ tsp of Himalayan pink salt, then drain. For the crystallized nuts, mix all the ingredients in a bowl, making sure the nuts are evenly coated. Dehydrate at 45°C / 113°F for 12–24 hours, depending on how crunchy you want your nuts, or dry out in your oven set to the lowest temperature, checking them every half-hour or so until they are crunchy.

Line the base of a 18–20 cm (7–8 inch) loose-bottomed cake tin with baking parchment. Soak the figs for 30 minutes in filtered water then drain and cut off the tops. In a food processor, roughly chop the walnuts and pistachio nuts then set aside. Place the figs, vanilla seeds, salt and orange zest in the food processor and blend to form a paste. Add the chopped nuts and ground almonds (almond meal) and blitz once more until everything starts to stick together. Turn out the mix into the prepared tin and flatten it down to form an even base. Freeze.

To make the bitter orange ice cream, put all the ingredients, including the drained and rinsed nuts, in a blender and blend until completely smooth. There will be a very slight graininess from the nuts, but this will not be detected in the finished frozen cake. Pour out 310 g (11 oz / a third) of the mix onto the frozen base to make the first orange ice cream layer. Freeze until it has set, about 2–3 hours. Pour out another 310 g (11 oz / another third) of the ice cream mix and set aside. Leave the last third of the mix in the blender to make the chocolate orange ice cream and add the cacao powder, dates, salt and coconut milk. Blend until smooth.

When the first orange layer has set, melt the chocolate in a bain-marie (see page 156) and paint a thin layer over the frozen orange ice cream using a pastry brush. This adds a crunch and makes the cake look even more impressive when sliced into. Pour over the chocolate orange layer and return to the freezer for 2–3 hours. Repeat the process with another layer of melted chocolate and the final layer of orange ice cream. Freeze until set or overnight.

To make the glaze, place the melted coconut oil in a blender with the maple syrup, cacao, vanilla and salt and blend until smooth. Finally add the water and blend once more. Pour the mix out and set aside somewhere cool until needed.

To glaze, remove the cake from the freezer. Using a little hot water or a blow torch, warm the edges of the tin and then slide a knife around to loosen the cake. Demould the cake and remove the base of the tin. Place the cake on a wire rack with a tray fitted below it to catch excess glaze. If the glaze has set, heat it very slowly in a saucepan until just liquid and warm to touch. Using a ladle, pour the glaze over the cake, working quickly to get an even smooth layer. Tip the cake slightly to help if necessary, letting the glaze fall over the edges. Any leftover glaze can be warmed and served alongside the cake. Top with the crystallized nuts and serve immediately. Keeps in the freezer for at least three months.

# Blueberry lemon mousse cake with scented geranium flowers

*Serves 10–12*

### Filling

1 x 400 ml (14 fl oz) can coconut milk
150 g (5¼ oz / 1⅛ cup) cashew nuts
325 g (11½ oz / scant 2¼ cups)
   blueberries
Finely grated zest of 2 lemons
100 ml (3½ fl oz / ⅓ cup plus 1 tbsp)
   lemon juice
110 g (4 oz / ⅓ cup) raw clear honey
¼ tsp Himalayan pink salt
75 g (2¾ oz / ⅓ cup) coconut oil

### Vanilla base

90 g (3 oz / scant ⅔ cup) pitted Medjool
   dates
¼ tsp Himalayan pink salt
1 vanilla pod (bean), split lengthways
   and seeds scraped out
70 g (2½ oz / ¾ cup plus 2 tbsp)
   desiccated coconut
35 g (1¼ oz / ¼ cup) hemp seeds
30 g (1 oz / generous 2 tbsp) coconut oil

### Decoration

150 g (5¼ oz / 1 cup) blueberries
Scented geranium flowers or other
   edible flowers

*Whipped coconut cream lifts up this dessert to amazingly light and gorgeously smooth dimensions. It is rich and fresh at the same time, rounded out with the other-worldly scents of the fresh scented geranium flowers.*

The night before making this, place the can of coconut milk in the fridge. Line the base and sides of a 23 cm (9 inch) springform or loose-bottomed cake tin with baking parchment.

Soak the cashew nuts in 300 ml (10½ fl oz / 1¼ cups) of filtered water with ½ tsp of Himalayan pink salt for 3–4 hours.

To make the base, in a food processor chop up the dates with the salt and vanilla seeds to form a ball-like paste. Add the coconut and hemp seeds and blitz to combine. Melt the coconut oil, add to the mix and process until everything is combined. Turn out into the prepared tin and press down to form an even base. Refrigerate.

In a blender, process 150 g (5¼ oz / 1 cup) of the blueberries, the lemon zest and juice, honey and salt to form a purple juice. Drain and rinse the cashew nuts thoroughly, then add them to the blueberry juice and process until smooth.

Open the can of coconut milk and remove the cream on the top, which will have set overnight. You need 240 g (8½ oz / 1 cup), so use some of the thinner milk from the bottom of the can if necessary. Whip up the coconut cream in a freestanding mixer or using an electric whisk, until smooth and thick.

Melt the coconut oil and blend it into the blueberry juice and then add everything in the blender to the whipped coconut cream. Lightly whisk everything once more until just combined. If you overmix, the cake won't be as light as it should be. Fold in the remaining 175 g (6 oz / scant 1¼ cups) of blueberries then pour the mix over the prepared base. Refrigerate for about 2 hours until firm.

When set, demould. Decorate with blueberries and scented geranium flowers. Serve immediately. Keeps well in the fridge for up to five days.

Chocolates, petit fours
and little clean treats

# Homemade chocolate

*This is proper dark (bittersweet) chocolate with no added flavourings, emulsifiers or powders. It's rich and intense so best enjoyed in small pieces, letting it melt in your mouth to truly appreciate its pure flavour. To create a smooth chocolate with a glossy finish and a good 'snap' when broken, it is important to achieve the right 'temper'.*

*Makes about 450 g (1 lb) chocolate/ 5 x 90 g (3 oz) bars*

250 g (8¾ oz/1⅛ cup) cacao butter, chopped or processed into small pieces

125 g (4½ oz/1 cup plus 1 tbsp) cacao powder

90 g (3 oz/generous ¼ cup) maple syrup

1 vanilla pod (bean), split lengthways and seeds scraped out

### Suggested toppings and flavourings

*Wonder berry bar*
Goji berries, white mulberries, Incan berries, buckwheat groats, hulled hemp seeds and pumpkin seeds

*Exotic bar*
Dried mango, dried pineapple, toasted coconut flakes and cacao nibs

*Fruit 'n' nut 1*
Chopped dried unsulphured apricots and figs, raisins, Brazil nuts and almonds

*Fruit 'n' nut 2*
Pistachio, hazelnut, dried cranberry and dried blueberry

*Peppermint*
Add 1 tsp pure unsweetened peppermint extract to 90 g (3 oz) chocolate, then fill the mould

*Bitter orange*
Add 1 tsp pure unsweetened orange extract to 90 g (3 oz) chocolate, fill the mould, then decorate with cacao nibs

*Rose, orange blossom, raspberry, macadamia and sesame*
Add a generous ½ tsp rosewater and ½ tsp orange blossom water to 90 g (3 oz) chocolate, pour into the mould and then decorate with freeze dried raspberries, macadamia nuts and white sesame seeds

Line a large 35 x 25 x 2 cm deep (13¾ x 9¾ x ¾ inch) tray with baking parchment.

Make a bain-marie by fitting a glass or ceramic bowl over a saucepan of water. Do not let the bottom of the bowl touch the actual water. Bring the water to the boil then turn it down to a simmer. Very slowly melt the cacao butter in the bowl of the bain-marie. Take the cacao butter to no higher than 40–45°C/104–113°F. If you think it is getting too hot but hasn't all melted, take it off the heat to finish melting. It is important not to overheat it or the chocolate will taste grainy and be 'bloomed', with a white cloudy appearance.

When the cacao butter has melted and is at around 40–45°C/104–113°F, add the rest of the ingredients. This should lower the temperature and we now want to bring it down to 28–30°C/82–86°F; just above or below will be fine.

Blend all the ingredients together with a hand-held blender to get rid of any cacao powder lumps and until velvety smooth and glossy. Do not over-blend or the chocolate will stiffen too much. If it is too stiff, place the bowl back over the hot water and stir gently for a minute or so then remove from the heat. Keep stirring the chocolate gently to cool it then, when around 28–30°C/82–86°F, pour it into the lined tray. Bang the tray on a surface and shake it gently to get rid of any air bubbles and make a nice even layer of chocolate, then refrigerate.

Break up the set chocolate and store in a large glass jar or container in the fridge, where it will keep for at least three months.

# Make your own chocolate bars

*Homemade chocolate bars make the best edible gifts! I have given you my favourite toppings and flavourings, but add whatever you like to your real chocolate.*

You need chocolate moulds measuring 15 x 7 x 1 cm deep (6 x 2¾ x ⅓ inch). Wash the moulds with hot water, soap and a soft cloth, then dry with a cloth and polish with cotton wool before each use.

Make or melt the amount of homemade chocolate you want to use in a bain-marie (see above). Once the chocolate is around 28–30°C/82–86°F, pour or ladle it into the moulds, one at a time. Each bar (with above dimensions) can take 90 g (3 oz) of chocolate. Shake the moulds slightly and bang them a few times to get rid of any air bubbles and make an even layer. Next, if you want to, add 40–50 g (1½–1¾ oz) of toppings (see left for suggestions) and transfer to the fridge immediately to set. If you are in a rush, place in the freezer. Once set, the bars will fall out easily from the moulds.

# Dark (bittersweet) chocolate truffles

*All the dark (bittersweet) chocolate truffle recipes make about 40 truffles. They can be stored for a week in the fridge in an airtight container and are best served cold.*

**Dark (bittersweet) chocolate truffles**

125 g (4½ oz/6 tbsp) maple syrup

80 g (2¾ oz/⅔ cup) cacao powder, plus extra for coating

100 ml (3½ fl oz/⅓ cup plus 1 tbsp) coconut milk

2 tsp vanilla extract

Pinch Himalayan pink salt

80 g (2¾ oz/⅓ cup plus 1 tbsp) coconut oil

Combine all the ingredients, except the coconut oil, in a blender and blend until smooth. Melt the coconut oil and add to the blender, blending everything once more until completely smooth. Pour the ganache into a bowl, cover with baking parchment to the surface and refrigerate for 30 minutes or until firm to the touch. Remove from the fridge and shape small amounts of ganache between two teaspoons. For round truffles, roll the ganache between the palms of your hands. Roll in cacao powder to finish and refrigerate.

## Espresso truffles

**Espresso truffles**

1½ tbsp good-quality ground coffee

150 ml (5 fl oz/⅔ cup) boiling water

125 g (4½ oz/6 tbsp) maple syrup

70 g (2½ oz/½ cup plus 2 tbsp) cacao powder, plus extra for coating

80 g (2¾ oz/⅓ cup plus 1 tbsp) coconut oil

Pinch Himalayan pink salt

Combine the coffee and boiling water to make a strong coffee. Leave to brew. Strain through a small sieve to get 140 ml (5 fl oz/½ cup plus 4 tsp) of coffee. Combine the coffee, maple syrup and cacao powder in a blender and blend until smooth. Melt the coconut oil and add to the blender with the salt, blending until completely smooth. Pour the ganache into a bowl, cover with baking parchment to the surface and refrigerate for about 30 minutes to 1 hour or until firm to the touch. Remove from the fridge and shape and finish the truffles as above.

## Nutmeg chilli cinnamon truffles

**Nutmeg chilli cinnamon truffles**

1 x recipe Dark (bittersweet) chocolate truffles (see above), just made

¼ tsp chilli flakes

About 4 cm (1½ inch) piece freshly grated cinnamon or ½–1 tsp ground cinnamon

½ whole nutmeg, grated

Pinch of paprika

Cacao powder, for coating

Blend all the ingredients except the cacao powder in a blender until completely smooth. Pour the ganache into a bowl, cover with baking parchment to the surface and refrigerate for about 30 minutes or until firm to the touch.

Remove from the fridge and shape and finish the truffles as above.

**Blackcurrant purée**

150 g (5¼ oz/1½ cups) blackcurrants, fresh or defrosted if frozen

25 ml (¾ fl oz/5 tsp) water

20 g (¾ oz/1 tbsp) raw honey or coconut nectar

½ tsp lemon juice

## Blackcurrant truffles

**Blackcurrant truffles**

120 ml (4 fl oz/½ cup) blackcurrant purée (see above)

70 g (2½ oz/½ cup plus 2 tbsp) cacao powder, plus extra for coating

125 g (4½ oz/6 tbsp) maple syrup

80 g (2¾ oz/⅓ cup plus 1 tbsp) coconut oil

Put all the ingredients for the blackcurrant purée in a food processor and blitz until as smooth as possible. Pass everything through a fine sieve, pressing as much through as possible to make at least 120 ml (4 fl oz/½ cup) of purée.

Combine the blackcurrant purée, cacao powder and maple syrup in a blender and blend until smooth. Melt the coconut oil and add to the blender, blending until completely smooth. Pour the ganache into a bowl, cover with baking parchment to the surface and refrigerate for 30 minutes to 1 hour or until firm to the touch. Remove from the fridge and shape and finish the truffles as above.

# 'White chocolate' truffles

*The 'white chocolate' truffle recipes make about 25 small truffles. They can be stored for at least a week in the fridge in an airtight container.*

**'White chocolate' truffles**

120 g (4¼ oz / generous ½ cup) cacao butter

80 g (2¾ oz / scant ⅓ cup) cashew butter (see page 26)

¼ vanilla pod (bean), split lengthways and seeds scraped out

Finely grated zest of ¼ lemon

45 g (1½ oz / 2¼ tbsp) raw clear honey

Melt the cacao butter in a bain-marie (see page 156). Pour the melted butter into a blender, add the rest of the ingredients and blend until completely smooth. Add the flavourings below to make 'white chocolate' truffles. If you have leftover 'white chocolate', pour it out onto a tray lined with baking parchment and refrigerate to set. Snap up and store in a glass jar for use in other recipes.

## Matcha sesame 'white chocolate' truffles

**Matcha sesame truffles**

½ x recipe 'White chocolate' truffles (see above), just made or melted

1½ tsp Matcha green tea

20 g (¾ oz / 1 tbsp) raw honey

1 tbsp cashew butter (see page 26)

Pinch Himalayan pink salt

**Shell**

½ x recipe 'White chocolate' truffles (see above), melted

30 g (1 oz / ¼ cup) white sesame seeds

15 g (½ oz / ⅛ cup) black sesame seeds

In a blender, blend all the truffle ingredients together until completely smooth. Pour into a bowl, cover to the surface with baking parchment and refrigerate for 15 minutes or until just firm.

Combine the white and black sesame seeds in a small bowl. Using a teaspoon, spoon out rounds of the truffle mix then roll them between your palms to make round truffles. Dip your fingers on one hand in the 'white chocolate' and spread it on your palms, then roll each truffle, one by one, in your palms, coating each truffle with white chocolate. Coat twice if necessary. When the chocolate is still wet, roll the truffles in the sesame seeds and leave to set.

## Camomile and honey 'white chocolate' truffles

**Camomile and honey truffles**

4 tbsp dried camomile heads, stalks removed

½ x recipe 'White chocolate' truffles (see above), just made or melted

1 tbsp cashew butter (see page 26)

20 g (¾ oz / 1 tbsp) raw honey

Pinch Himalayan pink salt

**Shell**

½ x recipe 'White chocolate' truffles (see above), melted

Sprinkling of dried camomile (see above)

In a spice grinder, grind all the camomile heads. Reserve ¼ of the ground camomile for sprinkling at the end. Add all the truffle ingredients to the blender and blend until smooth. Pour out into a bowl, cover to the surface with baking parchment and refrigerate for 15 minutes or until just firm.

Using a teaspoon, spoon out rounds of the mix then roll them between your palms to make round truffles. Dip your fingers on one hand in the remaining 'white chocolate' and spread it on your palms, then roll each truffle, one by one, in your palms, coating each truffle with white chocolate. Coat twice if necessary. When the chocolate is still wet, sprinkle the tops of the truffles with the reserved ground camomile.

### NOTES
*I prefer to use raw honey in these truffles as it really helps to enliven the flavours, but blonde coconut nectar also works as a vegan replacement.*

*All truffles, dark (bittersweet) chocolate and 'white', are suitable for freezing.*

***Previous spread from left to right:*** *Dark (bittersweet) chocolate, Espresso, Blackcurrant and Nutmeg chilli cinnamon truffles. Cut chocolates top to bottom – Hazelnut and lime rocher (see page 166) and Matcha sesame 'white chocolate' truffle. Boxed chocolates left to right – Camomile and honey 'white chocolate' truffles, Hazelnut and lime rochers and Matcha sesame 'white chocolate' truffles.*

# Cardamom, cranberry and pistachio mendiants

## Makes about 30 mendiants

½ x recipe 'white chocolate yogurt'
  (see page 104)
1 tsp ground cardamom
20 g (¾ oz / 1 tbsp) raw clear honey or
  blonde coconut nectar
25 g (¾ oz / 3 tbsp) pistachio nuts,
  preferably activated dried (see
  page 25)
½ tsp fleur de sel
25 g (¾ oz / scant ¼ cup) dried
  cranberries

*Mendiants are popular French petit fours, coin-shaped morsels encrusted with jewels in the form of nuts and dried fruits. Serve after a meal or wrap in pretty packaging to make delightful edible gifts. Do play around with the flavours, nuts and dried fruits.*

Preheat the oven to 170°C / 325°F / Gas Mark 3. Line two small baking trays with baking parchment.

Place the 'white chocolate yogurt' in a large bowl and stir in the cardamom and honey or coconut nectar. If you have just made the 'white chocolate yogurt' and it is very runny, leave to cool until just about to set. In the meantime, toast the pistachio nuts on one of the baking trays for 5–7 minutes until just getting colour, leave to cool then chop in half.

Place the cooled 'white chocolate' mix in a piping bag and cut a small hole in the end. If necessary, warm the mix inside the bag in the palms of your hands. Squeeze out about 2 cm (¾ inch) diameter rounds of 'white chocolate' onto the unused baking tray. While the chocolate is still wet, sprinkle each round with a little fleur de sel, top with a few pieces of cranberry and pistachio and transfer to the fridge to set. Serve straight from the fridge. These will keep for at least a week in a sealed container in the fridge.

# Fresh mint thins

## Makes about 50 mint thins

100 g (3½ oz) homemade chocolate
  (see page 156) or dark (bittersweet)
  chocolate 85% cocoa solids
Large bunch fresh mint leaves

*With only two ingredients, these are very simple to make but are extremely yummy. A thin layer of dark (bittersweet) chocolate snaps to reveal a refreshing real mint leaf centre. Just make sure that the chocolate is at the right temperature for dipping. Serve these after supper or as sweet canapés, with fresh mint tea or strong coffee.*

Place a tray lined with baking parchment or a piece of marble lined with baking parchment in the freezer before you start. Melt the chocolate using a bain-marie (see page 156). Keep the chocolate at 28–32°C (82–89°F) for best results. Pluck all the mint leaves off the large stalks, leaving the small stalks on each leaf so they can be held while dipping the leaf. Reserve the end sprigs for use in smoothies or salads.

Remove the tray or marble from the freezer. Lower each leaf, one at a time, into the chocolate, coating the whole leaf well, then place on the chilled tray or marble. If the chocolate is at 28–32°C (82–89°F) you should get a good coating, but dip the leaf again if necessary. The fresh mint is strong so it's best to have a good layer of chocolate covering it.

Allow the chocolate to set, either in a cool place or in the fridge, then carefully remove the leaves from the tray or marble and store until needed in the fridge. These are best eaten fresh or on the following day.

# Adzuki bean Brazil nut fudge

*Makes about 35 x 2.5 cm (1 inch) square pieces*

100 g (3½ oz / generous ½ cup) dried adzuki beans (about 215 g (7½ oz / scant 1 cup) cooked weight)
500 ml (17 fl oz / 2⅛ cup) filtered water
220 ml (7½ fl oz / scant 1 cup) sweet thick cashew milk (see page 28)
2 tbsp cacao powder
3 tsp carob powder
1 tsp maca powder
1 tsp lucuma powder
½ tsp Himalayan pink salt
2 tsp vanilla extract
120 g (4¼ oz / generous ¾ cup) pitted Medjool dates, or dates soaked in filtered water for 1 hour then drained
75 g (2¾ oz / ⅓ cup) coconut oil, melted
10 g (⅓ oz / ½ tbsp) date syrup, optional
80 g (2¾ oz / generous ⅓ cup) Brazil nuts, roughly chopped

**For dusting**
½ tsp cacao powder
1 tsp carob powder
¼ tsp maca powder
¼ tsp lucuma powder

*This may be the most healthy and delicious fudge that you will ever taste! It is sublimely soft and creamy with malty chocolate-caramel notes from the combination of the carob, maca and lucuma with the cacao. Enjoy it as an afternoon pick-me-up with a cup of tea or serve after a meal.*

Soak the adzuki beans for 12 hours or overnight in 300 ml (10½ fl oz / 1¼ cups) of filtered water. Line a small baking tin that is at least 2.5 cm (1 inch) deep with baking parchment. I use a 30 x 20 cm (12 x 8 inch) brownie tin and the fudge fills half the tin.

Strain and refresh the soaked beans and place in a saucepan with the measured filtered water. Bring to the boil, then lower the heat to medium and continue cooking for 25–30 minutes, until soft and very slightly al dente, drain and rinse.

Place the cashew milk in a blender with the cacao, carob, maca, lucuma, salt and vanilla and blend until smooth. Scrape down the blender and repeat if necessary. Add the dates to the blender and blitz on high speed for about 20 seconds. You will need to scrape down the mixture about three times until almost totally smooth, but don't worry if you have a few lumps.

Once smooth, add the cooked beans, alternating with the coconut oil. Start on the slowest speed and gradually increase to full speed, scraping down the mix a couple of times – it will take about 5 minutes to become smooth. Then taste the fudge. I like it as it is, but if you want it a little sweeter, add the date syrup and blend once more.

Scrape the fudge into a large bowl and combine with the Brazil nuts, then spread out evenly in the lined tray to a thickness of about 2.5 cm (1 inch). Chill for 3 hours in the fridge or preferably overnight, as it will then be firmer and easier to cut as it is quite a soft fudge. When set, cut into 2.5 cm (1 inch) cubes with a sharp knife. Mix together the cacao, carob, maca and lucuma powders and sieve over the top of the fudge. The fudge will keep in the fridge for at least three days or in the freezer for up to one month.

**NOTES**
*The Brazil nuts add a lovely crunch, but feel free to use other nuts and even dried fruits; or leave them all out and keep it delightfully smooth.*

*The malty chocolate mixture made before you add the beans, oil and nuts can be used to make delicious drinks. Add your favourite plant-based milk for an indulgent superfood-boosting smoothie, or warm it up with extra milk, a pinch of cinnamon and chilli to make a decadent hot chocolate.*

# Dream coconut ice

**Makes 35–40 squares**

1 whole coconut, to get about 260 g
(9¼ oz) grated flesh and coconut water
60 ml (2 fl oz / ¼ cup) coconut milk
100 ml (3½ fl oz / ⅓ cup plus 1 tbsp)
coconut water (using water from the
coconut first)
½ tsp vanilla extract
40 g (1½ oz / 2 tbsp) raw clear honey
Pinch Himalayan pink salt
70 g (2½ oz / ⅓ cup) coconut oil

*When my Malaysian friend, Grace, mentioned using fresh coconut in my coconut ice, as opposed to dried desiccated coconut, I knew she was on to something. Fun as well as elegant, these light cubes of intense coconut flavour delicately sweetened with a little honey are perfect for children and adults alike.*

Line a 20 x 16 x 2 cm deep (8 x 6 x ¾ inch) rectangular baking tin (or similar sized square tin) with baking parchment.

Grate the coconut using a box grater. Place half of it, 130 g (4½ oz), in a saucepan with the rest of the ingredients, except the coconut oil, and heat, bringing just to a boil. Add the coconut oil and keep the mix on a low boil for about 10 minutes, until most of the milk and water have been absorbed and you are left with mainly melted oil. Add the remaining coconut and stir in thoroughly.

Pour the mix into your prepared tray and press it in, compacting it well. You want it to be no more than 1 cm (⅓ inch) thick. Refrigerate for 1 hour or until firmly set, remove from the tin carefully and cut up into 35–40 squares with a sharp serrated knife. This is best eaten fresh, but it will last in the fridge for three to five days, depending on the freshness of the coconut.

**VARIATION**

*Toasted Coconut Ice Cups*
To get that delicious toasted coconut flavour, I often make half of the mix into these wonderful coconut cups. Simply take pieces of the mix, compact it in your hands, and put into mini cake cases. Bake for 8–10 minutes on 170°C / 325°F / Gas Mark 3 or until the tops are golden brown. Leave to cool and set then serve.

# Hazelnut and lime rochers

**Makes about 30 rochers**

100 g (3½ oz / ¾ cup) hazelnuts,
preferably activated dried (see
page 25)
200 g (7 oz) homemade chocolate
(see page 156) or dark (bittersweet)
chocolate 85% cocoa solids
100 g (3½ oz / ⅓ cup plus 1 tbsp)
hazelnut butter (see page 26)
40 g (1½ oz / 2 tbsp) raw honey or
coconut nectar
Finely grated zest and 1 tsp juice of ½
lime
Pinch Himalayan pink salt

*Crunchy toasted hazelnuts coated in dark (bittersweet) chocolate surrounding a soft praline centre with a hint of lime, these are some seriously sophisticated petit fours.*

Preheat the oven to 180°C / 350°F / Gas Mark 4 and line a baking tray with baking parchment. Place the hazelnuts on the lined baking tray and toast for 6–8 minutes. Leave to cool, remove the skins then roughly chop in a food processor until small pieces, but not ground. Set aside on a plate.

Melt the chocolate slowly in a bain-marie (see page 156). Once melted, remove 60 g (2 oz / ¼ cup) and in a bowl combine it with the hazelnut butter and honey to form a smooth paste. Add the lime zest, juice and salt and stir once more. Using two teaspoons, make about 30 small rounds. Roll into balls. Check the remaining melted chocolate is at 28–30°C / 82–86°F. Dip all the balls, one at a time on a fork, into the chocolate then roll in the chopped nuts. Finish by coating your palms in chocolate and rolling each of the balls in your palms to coat with chocolate. Leave on a piece of baking parchment to set, repeat with the rest of the balls and then refrigerate. Will keep in the fridge for up to ten days. (Illustrated on pages 158–9.)

# Puff-me-up clusters

*Movie nights just got a whole lot better with these amazingly tasty good-for-you treats: crunchy popcorn tossed in peanut butter caramel plus nutty puffed quinoa with bittersweet chocolate and crunchy almonds, both with delectable sweet and salty notes. These are irresistible, so watch out, they'll be gone in a flash.*

## Peanut butter caramel popcorn clusters

*Serves 6–8*

½ tbsp coconut oil
4 tbsp popcorn kernels
4 tbsp coconut sugar
5 tbsp maple syrup
4 tbsp peanut butter
1 tsp coarse sea salt, finely ground

Line a large tray with baking parchment. In a medium–large lidded saucepan, melt the coconut oil, add the popcorn and put the lid on the saucepan. Keep the lid on until all of the popping has stopped, shaking the saucepan around a little as it pops so that it doesn't burn. Place the popped corn into a bowl.

In the same saucepan, melt the coconut sugar, maple syrup, peanut butter and salt until smooth and just starting to bubble. Add the popcorn, remove from the heat and keep stirring until all the corn is coated. Transfer onto a tray, leave to cool slightly and then break up into clusters or individual pieces.

These are best eaten fresh but will keep in a sealed bag or container for up to three days.

## Dark (bittersweet) chocolate chip, salted almond and puffed quinoa clusters

*Serves 6–8*

70 g (2½ oz / ½ cup) almonds, preferably activated dried (see page 25)
½ tsp coarse sea salt, finely ground
70 g (2½ oz) homemade chocolate (see page 156) or dark (bittersweet) chocolate 85% cocoa solids
70 g (2½ oz / generous ¼ cup) almond butter (see page 26)
6 tbsp quinoa puffs
20 g (¾ oz / 1 tbsp) maple syrup

Preheat the oven to 180°C/350°F/Gas Mark 4. Line a baking tray or regular tray, about 30 x 20 cm (12 x 8 inches), with parchment paper.

Line another baking tray with baking parchment, spread out the almonds and toast for 6–8 minutes or until they are just starting to colour. Remove from the oven, cool slightly then roughly chop and toss in a bowl with the salt.

Roughly chop 20 g (¾ oz) of the chocolate and add it to the almonds, along with the almond butter, quinoa puffs and maple syrup and stir. Melt the rest of the chocolate in a bain-marie (see page 156) and pour it over the mix, combining everything together.

Pick up pieces of the mix in your fingertips, making them into rough clusters. Place the clusters onto the lined tray and refrigerate for a few minutes to set the chocolate then serve.

These are best eaten fresh but will keep in a sealed bag or container for at least one week.

# Lemon, strawberry and Earl Grey friands with lemon drizzle

......................................................................................................

*These light and fresh lemon sponge morsels burst with juicy, plump strawberries while the delicate fragrant Earl Grey flavour lingers on your taste buds. I like to serve them at summer tea parties or for pudding with fresh berries and natural yogurt or ice cream. You can use other berries such as blueberries and raspberries, or experiment with different teas, ground dried petals, or spices.*

......................................................................................................

## Makes 16 friands

### Friands

90 g (3 oz / ⅓ cup plus 1 tbsp) non-hydrogenated dairy-free butter

75 g (2¾ oz / ½ cup plus 1 tbsp) agave sugar

15 g (½ oz / 1½ tbsp) brown rice flour

15 g (½ oz / 2 tbsp) sorghum flour

1 tbsp arrowroot

3 tsp Earl Grey tea leaves, finely ground in a spice grinder

3 egg whites (120 g / 4¼ oz / scant ½ cup)

¼ tsp Himalayan pink salt

75 g (2¾ oz / ⅔ cup) ground almonds (almond meal)

Zest of ½ lemon, finely grated

16 small or 4 large strawberries, quartered, about 125 g (4½ oz)

### Glaze

2–2½ tsp lemon juice

6 tbsp agave sugar, sifted

Preheat the oven to 180°C / 350°F / Gas Mark 4. Melt the butter and brush a little of it over the friand moulds (or a fairy cake tin) to grease them. Put the rest of the butter to one side.

Sieve together the agave sugar, flours and arrowroot. Mix in the ground Earl Grey. Whisk the egg whites with the salt until light and firm using a hand-held whisk or freestanding mixer. Lightly fold the flour mix and tea into the whisked egg whites, followed by the ground almonds (almond meal) and lemon zest. Finish by carefully folding in the melted butter until everything is just incorporated, but do not overmix.

Using a teaspoon, divide the mix between the friand moulds. Do not overfill the moulds – leave a few millimetres (⅛ inch) between the top of the mix and the mould. Finish each cake with a small strawberry or quarter of a large strawberry, pressed down into the mix.

Bake for 10–12 minutes, rotating the tray after 5–6 minutes, until the friands are light golden brown and firm but light to touch. Leave to cool for about 10 minutes, then remove from the mould and leave to cool on a wire rack.

To make the glaze, stir the lemon juice into the agave sugar until smooth. Spoon teaspoons of the glaze onto the friands, picking them up and turning with your hands so that the glaze just falls over the edges. Serve immediately. The glaze does sink in after a while but the friands will still have a lovely shiny finish.

Serve with a cup of Earl Grey tea made with a slice of lemon. These are best eaten fresh, but will keep for up to three days in an airtight container.

### NOTE

*This is the only recipe in this book in which I use agave sugar. The traditional recipe for friands calls for icing (confectioner's) sugar to create their characteristic light texture. To achieve that texture with an alternative sweetener, I found agave sugar worked best. It also does not mask the delicate lemon and Earl Grey flavours. However, in the rest of my cooking, I prefer to stick to other sweeteners, as on pages 12–13. If you prefer not to use agave, you can replace it with raw honey, though the friands will be slightly less sweet.*

# Honeybee madeleines

*Made with honey and coconut sugar to give them a slight caramel crust and a mellow sweetness, these are utterly blissful morsels. As light as fairies and with a wholesome note from the slightly nutty flours, serve them straight from the oven to truly appreciate them at their best. A cup of tea is the perfect accompaniment.*

**Makes 12–16**

110 g (4 oz / ½ cup) non-hydrogenated dairy-free butter, plus extra for greasing, both melted
55 g (2 oz / ⅓ cup) brown rice flour
55 g (2 oz / scant ½ cup) sorghum flour
1 tsp baking powder
2 eggs
Pinch Himalayan pink salt
80 g (2¾ oz / scant ⅔ cup) coconut sugar
20 g (¾ oz / 1 tbsp) raw honey

Preheat the oven to 180°C / 350°F / Gas Mark 4. With a pastry brush, grease a madeleine tray (or fairy cake tin) with a little of the melted dairy-free butter. Sieve together the flours with the baking powder.

In a freestanding mixer, whisk the eggs and salt, starting from a slow speed and then gradually increasing to a high speed, until they are frothy and firm. Add the sugar and honey and continue whisking until just combined. Change the whisk to a paddle and alternately mix in the flours and melted butter until everything is just combined and well emulsified. Chill the mix in the fridge for at least 4 hours or overnight, covered to the surface with cling film (plastic wrap).

Give the mix a stir then pour it into a piping bag and cut a 1.5 cm (½ inch) diameter hole at the end. If the hole is too small, air will be lost from the mix when it is piped. Fill each madeleine mould, leaving a few millimetres (⅛ inch) at the top for the cakes to rise. Stop the mix from coming out of the piping bag by blocking the hole with two fingertips after filling each madeleine. You can spoon the mix in if you find it easier, just be careful not to knock too much air out of the mix.

Bake for 8–10 minutes until golden brown and the cakes just spring back when touched lightly. Leave to cool for about a minute, demould carefully, using a knife if necessary, and serve *straight* from the oven!

# INDEX

# STOCKISTS, BIBLIOGRAPHY AND ACKNOWLEDGEMENTS

## STOCKISTS

Although there is an array of brands available, here are some of my favourites. Supermarkets and healthfood shops should stock most of the ingredients used in my recipes. If there are any you can't find, online shops are very reliable and economical, particularly when buying in bulk. You can find out more about my producers, suppliers and their products on my blog www.henscleancakes.com.

**Aduna,** *www.aduna.com*. The highest-quality baobab and moringa powders.

**Biona Organic,** *www.biona.co.uk*. Date syrup, virgin coconut oil and butter, and apple cider vinegar.

**Coconom,** *www.coconom.com*. Organic, sustainably produced coconut sugar and coconut nectar syrup.

**Coyo,** *www.coyo.co.uk; www.coyo.us; www.coyo.com.au*. Dairy-free coconut yogurt; I use natural and chocolate.

**Doves Farm,** *www.dovesfarm.co.uk*. Gluten-free baking powder, bicarbonate of soda (baking soda), xanthan gum and some gluten-free flours.

**Hillfarm Oils,** *www.hillfarmoils.com*. Extra virgin cold pressed (EVCP) rapeseed oil.

**Hodmedod's,** *www.hodmedods.co.uk*. British-grown quinoa, beans and peas.

**Maldon Salt,** *www.maldonsalt.co.uk*. Coarse pure sea salt.

**Meridian,** *www.meridianfoods.co.uk*. Maple syrup, molasses and nut butters.

**SugaVida, a Conscious Food Company,** *www.sugavida.com*. Organic, sustainably produced and ethically traded Palmyra nectar powder.

**Pump Street Bakery,** *www.pumpstreetbakery.com*. Chocolate: I use 100% and 85% cocoa solids.

**Pure,** *www.puredairyfree.co.uk*. Non-hydrogenated dairy-free sunflower butter with no artificial colours or preservatives.

**Rainbow Wholefoods,** *www.rainbowwholefoods.co.uk*. Stock many of the ingredients used in *Clean Cakes*.

**Rude Health,** *www.rudehealth.com*. Plant-based milks such as almond and hazelnut, gluten-free sprouted oats and sprouted buckwheat flour.

**St Dalfour,** *www.stdalfour.co.uk; www.stdalfour.com.au*. All natural 100 per cent fruit preserves with no added cane sugar.

**Shipton Mill,** *www.shipton-mill.com*. Outstandingly high-quality wholegrain gluten-free organic flours. Or use **Bob's Red Mill,** *www.bobsredmill.com,* in the USA.

**Steenbergs Organic,** *www.steenbergs.co.uk*. Pure extracts, such as vanilla, orange and lemon and peppermint, and flower waters as well as spices.

**Teapigs,** *www.teapigs.co.uk; www.teapigs.com; www.tea-pigs.com.au*. Chai-tea, powdered Matcha green tea and other interesting infusions.

## OTHER USEFUL STOCKISTS AND WEBSITES

*www.detoxyourworld.com*
*www.eattheseasons.co.uk*
*www.ethicalsuperstore.com*
*www.goodnessdirect.co.uk*
*www.planetorganic.com*
*www.suma.coop*

## BIBLIOGRAPHY

In 2014, I passed the Institute of Optimum Nutrition Home Study Course. The following material helped me greatly with my understanding of many of the subjects covered in my book, notably gluten, grains, dairy and refined sugar:
*Patrick Holford's New Optimum Nutrition Bible*, Patrick Holford, Piatkus, 2004
*The Concise Human Body Book*, Steve Parker, Dorling Kindersley, 2009
*The Complete Guide to Nutritional Health*, Pierre Jean Cousin and Kirsten Hartvig, Duncan Baird Publishers, 2004

## CREDITS

Chad Robertson and Tartine Bakery for inspiring my Dark (bittersweet) chocolate dipped peanut butter and jelly dreams on page 94 and my Rosemary, orange, dark (bittersweet) chocolate and hazelnut sablés on page 93; and to Diana Henry for inspiring my Clementine and pomegranate jewel cake on page 40.

## ACKNOWLEDGEMENTS

Writing this book has been a dream come true so I would like to say a huge thank you to Jacqui for giving me the chance to do it. Thank you to Fritha, Rachel and Claire for making my vision become a reality; to Lisa for your beautiful photography and Fiona for all your help on shoot days. Thank you to friends, family and local villagers, my chief recipe-testers; to Rosemary and Caroline for your endless supply of stunning flowers and extra props and to Wendy for always being there. A huge thanks to everyone who has helped me get where I am today – old colleagues who taught me so much; all those who have supported my work, in Suffolk and beyond, and those who wholeheartedly supported my new business, Hen's Clean Cakes. I look forward to deepening my knowledge of these wonderful ingredients and sharing more of my food with you through the recipes on my blog and at future events. To my brother and sister, thank you for always encouraging me in everything that I do. And lastly, none of this would have been possible without my parents to whom I am eternally grateful for your undying support, patience, generosity and love. This book is dedicated to you.